THE GENERIC CHALLENGE

THE GENERIC CHALLENGE

Understanding Patents, FDA and
Pharmaceutical Life-Cycle Management

Martin A. Voet, B.S., M.B.A., J.D.

BrownWalker Press
Boca Raton 2005

The Generic Challenge: Understanding Patents, FDA and Pharmaceutical Life-Cycle Management

Copyright © 2005 Martin A. Voet

BrownWalker Press
2005
Boca Raton, Florida • USA

ISBN: 1-58112-430-9 *(paperback)*
ISBN: 1-58112-432-5 *(ebook)*

BrownWalker.com

DISCLAIMER

This book is intended to provide information about the subject matter covered. It is sold with the understanding that the publisher and author are not engaged in rendering legal services or providing legal advice. If legal advice is required, the services of a competent legal adviser should be obtained.

Reasonable efforts have been made to make this book accurate and complete. However, there may be mistakes, both typographical and in content. Therefore, this text should be used only as a general guide and is not to be relied on in any particular, keeping in mind that laws and interpretation of rules change over time.

The purpose of this little book is to educate and inform. The author and publisher shall have neither liability nor responsibility to any person or entity with respect to any loss or damage caused or alleged to be caused directly or indirectly by the information contained in this book.

The opinions expressed in this book are solely the personal opinions of the author in his individual capacity. Nothing in this book shall be attributable to the author in any representational capacity or to any other person or legal entity.

DEDICATION

This book is dedicated to the one I love...my beautiful, intelligent, caring, loving, kind, thoughtful and most wonderful wife and life companion of 39 years and counting, Robin Gay Voet.

ACKNOWLEDGMENT

I have not attempted to cite in the text all of the authorities and sources consulted in the preparation of this book. To do so would make the book cumbersome and probably unreadable to the non-professional. Besides, I wanted to write a simple book that would be easy to read and understand and by implication that means no footnotes.

Thanks also to friends and colleagues for offering suggestions for improvements and especially to my wonderful daughter-in-law, Melissa Voet, for assistance with proofreading.

I also want to thank my good friend and colleague, George Lasezkay, principal of Turning Point Consultants of Irvine, California for repeatedly encouraging me to write this book, whose genesis was a chapter outline sketched out on a pad at River Run in the spring skiing sunshine of Sun Valley, Idaho between ski runs on Baldy in the Spring of 2004.

ABOUT THE AUTHOR

Martin A. Voet is a Senior Vice President and Chief Intellectual Property Counsel for a Fortune 500 pharmaceutical company with over 20 years experience in intellectual property practice. He has degrees in chemistry, business and law and years of practical experience in patenting pharmaceutical products, litigating with generic companies over them and providing practical, hands-on planning for pharmaceutical life-cycle management.

He graduated from the University of California at Berkeley with a B.S. degree in Chemistry; received his M.B.A. degree from Pepperdine University School of Business and Management and was awarded a J.D. degree with honors from the George Washington University National Law Center.

He is a member of the State Bar of California, the American Intellectual Property Law Association and the Licensing Executives Society.

He has been a contributor to the Practicing Law Institute's *Global Intellectual Property* series and its annual *Patent Litigation* series. He is also a contributor and member of the Editorial Board of *Managing Intellectual Property*.

"The desire to take medicine is perhaps the greatest feature which distinguishes man from animals"

Sir William Osler, M.D.

PREFACE

A horse walks into a bar and the bartender says, "Why the long face?" Why indeed. The pharmaceutical industry should be on top of the world with innovative discoveries and development of so many fantastic new drugs for treating life-threatening illnesses, while often avoiding expensive surgeries. There are targeted new drugs for treating once deadly cancers and for preventing blindness; wondrous new life-saving biotech products for treating stroke and multiple sclerosis; amazing new lifestyle enhancement drugs from growing hair and erasing wrinkles to maintaining sexual vigor; yet the pharmaceutical industry is trashed nightly as being second only to the tobacco industry in the corporations-we-hate-most department.

Politicians sensing this are quick to lay blame, announce conspiracies, demand lower prices and push for re-importation of low-priced drugs from foreign countries. African countries blame them as if they started the AIDS epidemic, instead of coming up with promising treatments. Generic drugs are thought to be the answer to what is wrong with healthcare, while innovators are viewed at best with a jaundiced eye. In this charged and decidedly unfriendly environment, why write this book?

In fact, there is nothing wrong with generics and they are a valuable and necessary part of a good health care system. However, there would be no generics without the innovators and I am worried that the public has lost sight of this truism.

This book is intended to encourage the innovators to persevere in the face of this adversity and to redouble their efforts to innovate and to continue to see themselves as the valuable contributors to society that they are.

Martin A. Voet

December 3, 2004

Contents

Chapter 5

Drug Product Exclusivity 57

Chapter 6

Hatch Waxman Act 71

Chapter 7

Putting it All Together: Product Life-Cycle Management 85

Chapter 8

INTRODUCTION

The **Generic Challenge** is about providing the necessary information to pharmaceutical executives, managers, regulatory, legal and business development professionals, those involved in strategic marketing and in research and development, among others in the pharmaceutical field, to deal with the increasingly aggressive tactics of generic companies and that are designed to legally copy innovative drug products.

Generic drugs offer significant benefits to society and I am not advocating their abolishment. People need reasonably priced drugs. But people and their children also need new and better innovative drugs in the future. If the generic industry is not kept in check, the balance between the goals of low priced currently available drugs and innovative, life saving and life enhancing *future* drugs will not be maintained, and while we may have cheap drugs, we will have no new, innovative drugs.

Most people don't understand that new, innovative drugs are invented and developed by the drug industry without any significant help from the government. Sometimes the basic concepts are discovered at Universities and are licensed to the pharmaceutical companies at a very early stage in development, and once in a while something comes from a government-sponsored research institute such as the National Institutes of Health (NIH), but not very often. And even then, the long times and great costs and capital risks for development and approval by FDA are all on the pharmaceutical industry alone.

A significant percent of the profits made by the drug companies in marketing and selling their current drugs is plowed back into research to discover and develop future drugs. No profits on current drugs, no research on future drugs.

Generic companies have no expense for discovery or development or marketing of drugs. They are legally allowed to copy an innovator's drug after a relatively short time of exclusivity for the innovator, unless there is patent protection. If they can overcome the patent protection, they can legally obtain rights to use all the safety and efficacy data developed by the innovator and copy the drug. Then they only have to manufacture the drug and put it on the market. No payments are due to the innovator by the generic company for use of his property.

A comparable situation would be you building a house and putting a lock on the door and then after a period of time, anyone who can pick the lock can legally use your house. Well, you say, that's not fair. I built and paid for the house, no one should be able to use it just because they can pick the lock. You are right of course. No one would dream of that kind of legal process for houses. But that is precisely what happens in the wonderful world of pharmaceuticals where a generic company gets free use of your FDA drug file if he can pick the lock of your patent. In fact, current law actually gives generic companies *an incentive* to do so by providing a period of exclusivity for the first generic company that tries to pick a product's patent lock!

In the last 20 years since the Hatch Waxman Act fostered the generics industry, it has grown steadily so that now it accounts for over 50% of the drugs sold in America. Not satisfied with that enviable track record, during the last five years, the generic drug companies have adopted a "take no prisoners" attitude and are attacking virtually all new drug patents at the earliest possible time. Most pharmaceutical companies today have all of their important products under attack. (At a recent mandatory settlement conference, a generic company CEO informed me "We never settle".)

One of the main reasons for the ongoing consolidation of the pharmaceutical industry is the shortening of product life cycles caused by generic intrusion at an earlier and earlier time in the product life cycle. As the product life cycle gets shorter, simple economics suggests that the pharmaceutical industry may be forced to recover its long term investment over the shorter time period. This in turn leads to further political pressure for more generic drugs, more price reductions, calls for Canadian re-importation of drugs, price controls, etc...

We must be mindful of the fairy tale of the goose that laid the golden egg and not take the survival of the innovative pharmaceutical industry for granted. You may think I am being melodramatic here, but an actual case in point is Canada.

Canada decided some years ago that it preferred cheap drugs to future innovative drugs and established governmental policies to achieve that. There is no data protection in Canada for drug dossiers and the only thing between a new pharmaceutical product and its becoming a generic from day one is a patent. Even there the law is not very friendly to innovators and it is the policy of the health authorities to officially favor the generic industry. The net result is that there is virtually no innovative drug industry in Canada and like Blanche in *A Street Car Named Desire*, it depends on the kindness of strangers for future innovative drugs. If all countries took that approach, eventually, there would be no innovative pharmaceutical industry and no new innovative drugs.

The purpose of this book is to familiarize the reader with both the strategic and tactical aspects of the interaction of patents, FDA regulations and the Hatch Waxman Act on pharmaceutical product life cycles to provide the reader with the information necessary to successfully face **The Generic Challenge**.

However, this is not as easy as it may sound. Patent law tends to be an arcane specialty with its own jargon like "prior art", "terminal disclaimer" and "102 reference"; while FDA law, with its dense and almost impossible to understand regulations and its own jargon like "505(b)(2) filing" and "Phase III clinical trial", is not much better.

Furthermore, when you need an answer to a patent question, you ask a patent lawyer. If the question also involves FDA regulatory issues, you will generally be told that that is an area outside the expertise of the patent lawyer and you should consult an expert in FDA law or regulation. So you find such a person and they will tell you all you need to know about FDA law and regulations, but if the question also involves patents in any significant way, they will tell you it is outside their area of expertise, so please to consult a patent lawyer.

This Catch 22 problem for pharmaceutical managers and executives is that there are an increasing number of important "you bet your product" issues that depend on fully understanding how patent and regulatory laws and regulations and statutes such as the Hatch Waxman Act interact to influence the long-term success of a pharmaceutical product.

That means pharmaceutical managers and executives alike who want to succeed in their jobs have no choice but to become knowledgeable in these matters so that they can plan for the successful development and long term success of their company's pharmaceutical products. This book might also be helpful to the regulatory lawyer or patent lawyer (who can save time by skipping the chapter on his or her specialty) who wishes he or she had a better understanding of the interaction of patent law with regulatory law so that they can better see the bigger picture and help achieve the goal of successful pharmaceutical product life-cycle management.

This book is intended to explain those subjects in understandable language so that you, the reader, will be able to ask the right questions and understand the answers you receive. Keep in mind this book is not intended to be, nor could it be, a substitute for competent counsel in patent law and FDA regulatory matters, nor is it a substitute for expert consultants in pharmaceutical product life-cycle management.

The next three chapters are on patents. Chapter 1 is an **Overview of Patents**. Chapter 2 covers **Patent Enforcement and Infringement** and Chapter 3 describes **Pharmaceutical, Biological and Medical Device Patents**. These chapters provide the necessary basic background in patents for understanding pharmaceutical product life-cycle management. The next two chapters relate to regulatory matters. Chapter 4 is an **Overview of FDA** and chapter 5 covers **Drug Product Exclusivity**. These chapters provide the basics for understanding how these regulations and the available product exclusivities affect product life-cycle management. Chapter 6 discusses the final piece of the puzzle, the **Hatch Waxman Act**. Then Chapter 7 synthesizes the previous six chapters in **Putting it All Together: Product Life-Cycle Management**. Finally Chapter 8 closes with some **Conclusions and Final Thoughts**.

CHAPTER 1

Overview of Patents

The invention all admired,
and each, how he
To be the inventor missed,
so easy it seemed
Once found, which yet unfound
most would have
thought impossible.

John Milton
Paradise Lost

1. What is a Patent?

Patents have been around longer than you may think. They are even mentioned in the U.S. Constitution. Article I, Section 8 says "Congress shall have the Power ...to promote the Progress of Science and Useful Arts by securing for limited Times to Authors and Inventors the exclusive Right to their respective Writings and Discoveries."

Classically, a patent is described as a legal monopoly. We will find later that this description of a patent is not so accurate. Technically, a patent is a governmental grant that provides the holder for a limited period of time the exclusive right *to prevent others* from making, using or selling the patented product or process in exchange for his disclosure of the invention to the public. Notice we did *not* say the patent granted the *owner* the right to make, use or sell the invention (more on that later). Patents are intended to benefit the public, as they encourage less secrecy so that

1

important information is not lost when its owner dies, and to provide a means to encourage capital formation and investment in new ideas resulting in new industries, jobs, etc...

So now we know a patent is a time-limited right to exclude others from making, using or selling a product or process. So what is a "product" or "process"? The U.S. Supreme Court has broadly interpreted it as "anything under the sun made by man" when they agreed that the first man-made bacteria engineered to eat oil could be patented.

More specifically, a "product" can be a medical device such as an artificial heart or a composition of matter, such as a new chemical compound or biological agent, such as a vaccine, or formulation for a drug product or anything manufactured including a mouse genetically engineered to get cancer. A typical pharmaceutical product would consist of a patented chemical, known as a new chemical entity (NCE) and a patentable new formulation, such as an oral or topical dosage form, for delivery of the NCE to the body.

A "process" as applied to pharmaceutical products is a method of treatment of persons or materials to produce a given result. Included in patentable processes are methods of manufacturing a new chemical entity or a new method of manufacturing a known compound. A process is also a method of treating a condition or disease with either a new drug (first medical use) or an old drug that was previously known for treating a different condition or disease (second medical use).

The next sentence is the most important thing to know about patents. *A patent is a sword, not a shield.* That is, a patent is an offensive weapon that allows its owner, by enforcement of the patent in court, to prevent others from making the patented item or using or selling the patented method during the life of the patent. However, the patent has no defensive character and thus *it cannot protect you from being sued for infringement* under someone else's patent. Most people find this concept the most difficult one to understand. If I have a patent on my gizmo, how can I be sued for patent infringement? The answer is simple. A patent is a sword, not a shield. As mentioned earlier, a *patent does not grant its owner the right to do anything.* Instead, it grants the owner the right to *prevent others* from doing something.

For example, if I owned the patent for the first carburetor, which I designed to have two barrels, and later you improved my carburetor and obtained a patent on the first 4-barrel carburetor, what happens? I can keep your 4-barrel carburetor off the market with my general patent covering carburetors, but you can prevent me from selling your 4-barrel version of my carburetor with your patent. So if we both want to sell 4-barrel carburetors, we must cross license our patents to each other *or neither of us can sell them.* My broad carburetor patent does not shield me from your carburetor improvement patent and your improvement patent does not give you *any rights* to make your improvement.

Note that this dynamic system encourages others to make improvements on your invention so they can potentially negotiate entrance into the market. This technique of patenting improvements is practiced to the point of frustration in Japan where obtaining a patent can take 5-10 years and by the time the originator has patented the basic concept, there may be 20 patents in the hands of others covering a myriad of minor improvements. As a result, the patented article is difficult to make without running into one of the improvement patents thus forcing a cross-license.

2. Term of a Patent

In the U.S., patents used to have a term of 17 years from the date the patent was *granted.* This was set in stone. There were some exceptions, such as a shorter term caused by a terminal disclaimer (here comes that pesky jargon) where Patent Office rules require a patent owner to voluntarily agree to shorten his patent life in order to obtain the patent, but in general the rule was 17 years from date of grant. That was fair because if your patent application were held up in the Patent Office by government red tape, you would still get your 17 years once it was finally granted.

The rest of the world, on the other hand, gives 20 years from the date of *filing* the patent. This can allow quite a bit of mischief since it may take years to get the patent and any time lost in getting the patent is just hard luck for the patent owner. And competitors are happy to assist in any delays at the Patent Office through oppositions and other such procedures that allow competitors to challenge the grant of a patent. As a result it takes five to ten years to get a patent fully and finally granted in Europe and Japan, compared to one to three years in the U.S.

Then along came *harmonization*, a catchy word, but one that can lead to trouble. In the interests of harmonization, the U.S. agreed to match the other countries' rules so, effective June 8, 1995, any patents filed on or after that date had a life of 20 years from date of filing. Patents filed before that date got the longer of the two ways to compute their life (if only we all had that choice).

There was one catch and that was that the filing date the term of the patent was based on was the *earliest effective filing date* for the patent. This is because patent holders in the U.S. can file follow-on patent applications based entirely (continuations) or in part (continuations-in-part) on the former patent application and get the benefit of the date of filing of the first filed patent application for all common subject matter. If you file a string of patent applications as continuation applications or continuations-in-part (CIP) applications, the patent life for the last patent in the string is based on the filing date of the first patent. Of course, it is more complicated than that, with lots of rules and exceptions, but that is the basic story.

Typically, a patent attorney will use a continuation application to try to get claims granted in a follow-on patent application when time for prosecution before the Patent Office has run out on the originally filed application or when only some of the claims he or she wanted were granted in the originally filed application (thus a second bite at the apple). A continuation-in-part application is typically used to add something to an already existing application such as a new preferred formulation or some additional examples of compounds that were not disclosed in the original application.

Also in the interests of harmonization, the U.S. joined the international community in publishing patent applications 18 months after they are filed unless you ask not be published *and* agree not to file the patent outside the U.S. If you recall the beginning of the chapter where the granting of a patent was a reward for *disclosure* of the invention, there seems something basically wrong with forcing the disclosure of the invention without first granting the patent! But that is now the law and the only way to get around it is to agree not to file abroad.

(a) Submarine Patents

These new rules also solved a problem that had been invented by a man named Lemelson. Lemelson filed numerous patent applications in the 1950s on a variety of forward thinking concepts and then he did an unusual thing. Instead of being in a hurry to get his patents granted, he took his time and refiled the applications as continuation applications and kept adding subtle refinements to the claims and kept doing so *for 40 years* until, in the early 1990s when he finally allowed his patents to be granted, they covered important modern inventions. Since his patents were based on the old rules, he got a 17-year life from the date of grant.

After his patents were granted, he asked just about every company in the U.S. for royalties and got them after suing many. He collected over a *billion dollars* in royalties. His inventions ranged from Hot Wheels® track to bar coding (the black and white bars and numbers on just about every box of something sold today) and his patents covered something that just about every commercial enterprise did. He may have had more patents than Edison, but unlike Edison, he never actually made or perfected any of these inventions himself. (His patents did not ultimately do so well in court. For example, his Hot Wheels patent was held invalid on appeal reversing the $25 million damages judgment he was awarded by the lower court).

This kind of patent jokingly became known as a "submarine" patent because it stayed hidden under the surface for a long time and then arose and blasted you out of the water when you least expected it. That was because at the time, patent applications were kept secret in the U.S. until they were granted and he never filed his patents outside the U.S. where they would be published. By making the date of a patent based on its earliest effective filing date instead of its grant date, and by publishing pending patent applications, it essentially ended new submarine patents starting June 8, 1995.

Recently, courts have been ruling Lemelson's patents potentially unenforcible because of the way he got them, namely by intentional delay or as the courts have been calling it "late claiming". This is undoubtedly causing his successors some heartburn at their Aspen ski lodges, but presumably not Mr. Lemelson as he is undoubtedly too busy filing further continuing applications in the heavenly Patent Office.

So to recap, in the U.S., a patent having a filing date on or after June 8, 1995 has a term of 20 years from its earliest effective filing date. Patents filed before June 8, 1995 have a term which is the longer of 20 years from its earliest effective filing date or 17 years from its date of issue.

In the rest of the world, patents typically last 20 years from their filing dates. In Japan, patents are also granted for 20 years from their filing dates, but not longer than 15 years from their grant date. Patent terms can also be longer or shorter depending on several other factors.

A patent can have a shorter term if the patent holder agrees to shorten it. For example, one might agree to this due to a legal requirement to avoid a rejection on grounds of "double patenting". This involves having more than one patent covering essentially the same invention and may be allowed only if the later filed patent expires on the same date as the earlier filed patent (the so-called "terminal disclaimer".)

(b) Patent Term Extensions

A patent can also have a longer term based on certain delays in prosecution of the patent before the Patent Office that were caused by the Patent Office. It can also be longer for a pharmaceutical patent based on a *patent term extension* which may be granted based on national laws which provide additional life to make up for the time lost during drug registration. Typical patent term extensions are for up to five years in the U.S. and other similar patent term extensions are available in major countries such as Europe, Australia and Japan. Canada is an exception and allows no additional patent term. (Canada strongly favors generics to innovative pharmaceuticals so it is being consistent in not encouraging pharmaceutical research by refusing to allow extended terms for pharmaceutical patents.)

Patent term extensions do not actually extend the patent term for all of the claims of a patent. Instead, the patent term is extended only for the approved drug product. Thus a patent term extension will not keep competitors from filing for similar drugs to the innovator's drug after the nominal term of a patent, but it will help protect the approved drug product from becoming a generic drug.

The FDA takes the position that any subsequently approved drug containing the same active moiety as the approved drug product is also entitled to the patent term extension and indicates this in the Orange Book listing for the product. ("Active moiety" refers to the portion of the drug molecule that is active. Different salts, esters and hydrates of the same active drug contain the same active moiety.)

Patent term extensions are allowed only for patents that cover the first approval of a drug product and must be filed in the U.S. within six months of the date of the drug product approval if the patent has already been granted or within six months of the grant of the patent if the drug product is approved first. There is one exception to this. A patent for an approved veterinary drug product may be extended even if the same active drug moiety was previously approved for human use. In addition only one patent may be extended for an approved drug product and remaining patent life including extension cannot exceed 14 years.

3. How are Patents Obtained?

(a) First to Invent vs. First to File

Patents are typically filed first in one's home country. In the U.S. the first to *invent* is entitled to the patent while outside the U.S. the first to *file* a patent is awarded a patent if there is a dispute between inventors. If this conflict occurs, it is resolved in a proceeding called an "interference" in which each party tries to establish it invented first. Interferences occur in only about 1% of patents filed and are fought in the U.S. Patent and Trademark Office ("PTO") in a formal procedure which can be very expensive, time consuming and contentious. They also can be settled using a private arbitrator if both parties agree to do so, often with the understanding that the winner, whoever it is, licenses the loser. Outside the U.S., there is no need for such a procedure since the first to file always wins.

That puts the emphasis on prompt filing outside the U.S. and also inside the U.S. as the first to file has a significant advantage in an interference proceeding, because the second filer in time has the burden of proof to establish he is the first inventor. That means the first to file in the U.S. also will likely win the interference, unless the second to file can provide convincing evidence that he conceived the invention first and can also prove he was diligent in completing the invention from the time the first to file inventor filed until he filed.

One of the urban legends about patents is that the way for an inventor to prove his date of invention is to mail to himself a sealed envelope containing his invention disclosure to get a postmark establishing his date of invention. Some inventors tend to be secretive and even a little paranoid (in a good way) so they like this idea. The only problem is that such a procedure cannot establish a date of invention. That is because the patent laws provide that a date of invention can only be established if a third party, who is not an inventor, corroborates it. Typically, one does not even have to establish a date of invention as the issue usually comes up only if two different inventors are trying to claim the same invention at about the same time. So if you want to establish a date of invention, prepare a written disclosure of it and have a non-inventor read it and sign and date it. That establishes the required corroboration.

(b) Provisional Applications

The current trend in filing patents in the U.S. is to first file a *provisional* application because the governmental fees for filing are much less (currently $75) and it is not necessary to provide claims or other formalities. To perfect the provisional application, you must file a complete application within a year of the filing date of the provisional and you get the benefit of the earlier filing date of the provisional. You can file anything as a provisional application, such as a scientific paper, and use it as the basis of a patent application within the year provided. The only catch is that the provisional must provide the proper legal disclosure for a patentable invention in order to get the benefit of its filing date when you file the complete application later.

If you don't file the complete patent application within the year, the provisional dies in secret and has no further use. A bonus for filing the provisional application is that it does not count towards the life of the patent, so you really get 21 years from the filing date of a provisional patent application if you perfect it with a regular patent application filing within one year.

(c) Foreign Filings

Currently, the U.S. Patent Office publishes only complete applications within about 18 months of filing. Foreign patent applications are typically filed in foreign countries within 12 months of the date of first filing-whether it was a complete application or a provisional application. This is based on an international treaty (Paris Convention) that most countries belong to which provides that the first filing date of a patent becomes its effective filing date in all other countries so long as it is filed in those other countries within one year of its first filing anywhere.

In order to file outside the U.S., you must first obtain a license to do so from the U.S. Patent Office.

Licenses are automatically granted by the U.S. Patent Office after filing a patent application, unless your patent happens to relate to national security, atomic bombs, and the like. In the unlikely event you do not get the automatic license, it would not be wise to file abroad until you've seen your patent lawyer since your U.S. patent could be invalidated and you will likely have violated data security laws. If you do file abroad by mistake without a license, you can request a retroactive license if the subject matter is not of the kind to raise an issue and without having the FBI call for a chat.

(d) PCT

There is also another treaty (the Patent Cooperation Treaty or PCT) which allows a single place holder application to be filed within one year of the original filing date which reserves the right to file in most significant countries in the world (except currently Argentina and Taiwan) without having to actually file a patent application in each country until 31 months after the original filing date or 19 months after the PCT filing. This gives the inventor or his company more time to evaluate the invention without loss of any rights before having to file it worldwide at significant expense. It also typically provides enough time so that the patentability of the invention becomes clearer during prosecution of the patent in the home country Patent Office.

The rules are very unforgiving. If the 12-month foreign filing date is missed by even one day, the right to the earlier filing date is lost forever. If it is lost and if there was an intervening publication disclosing your invention between your U.S. filing date and your foreign filing date, your patent will not be valid. The PCT application is relatively inexpensive to file as foreign patent costs go (about $3,000) and it reserves your rights in all major countries worldwide. Remember that within about 6 months after filing the PCT it is published for all to see. If you want to keep your invention a secret until it is patented, don't file it abroad and don't file a PCT.

(e) Costs of Filing

Filing, obtaining and maintaining patents are not cheap. In addition to lawyer fees for preparation and prosecution before the Patent Office, there are governmental filing fees, examination fees, grant fees and periodic maintenance fees over the life of a patent. Current costs for obtaining a U.S. pharmaceutical patent including legal fees and government charges probably start at about $25,000: $5,000 to $15,000 for preparation and filing (though some can cost many times that), the same for examination, prosecution and grant and then three separate maintenance fees are due over the life of the patent totaling another $6,300.

In most foreign countries, the costs are generally higher due to translation costs and high government application and issue fees and annual maintenance fees over the life of the patent. "Small entities", individual inventors or companies with less than 500 employees and Universities also get a break on Patent Office fees, and are generally charged half the fees charged to large entities. The catch is that if and when a small entity becomes a large entity or licenses the patent to a large entity, normal fees are due from that time forward. This can be a trap for the unwary as fee mistakes can invalidate a patent.

4. Patent Contents

A patent consists of a multi-page printed document which gives the basic information about itself on the cover page which discloses the title of the patent, the name(s) and city address of the inventor(s) and the owner or assignee of the patent along with other useful information. In the U.S., the inventor is the owner unless the patent is assigned to another. If the patent has been assigned and that assignment has been recorded in the Patent Office, the patent will also set forth the name and city address of the assignee. The cover page also gives a summary of the invention, but it is written when the patent is filed and it is rarely changed, so it is a summary of the application when filed rather than a summary of the patent when granted, and therefore it may not accurately describe the invention claimed.

(a) Specification

The specification or body of the patent describes the invention and how it is to be used. It typically starts with a description of the field of the invention and describes what was known in the field before the invention was made, the so-called "prior art". It then describes the invention generally and then again in detail and offers examples of how it works. So if it is a patent on a new chemical entity (NCE), it will describe exactly how to make it and what the chemical and physical characteristics of the new compounds are. If it is about a new medical use, it will describe dosage forms, suitable formulations and concentrations of drug to be used and the disease or condition to be treated.

(b) Claims

At the end of the patent document are numbered paragraphs known as "claims". Claims are the heart and soul of a patent and define the rights granted to the patent holder as a deed to a piece of real property defines the metes and bounds of the property for the property owner. Litigation concerning a patent always focuses on the claims and each and every word in them. Skilled patent litigators often refer to infringers as *trespassers* on the *property* of the patent owner. So to understand a patent, you must first understand the claims.

The claims of a patent define the scope of the invention. Much time and attention is given to claims and that is what 95% of patent prosecution is about. When you submit the patent application, an Examiner reads it and must make a decision on whether to allow the claims you have presented to become part of a granted patent. Claims tend to get long winded because for some reason lost in the mists of time, there can only be one sentence in each claim, and so that sentence sometimes gets very long.

The broadest patents have the shortest claims. That is because the more you say about something, the more specific you become, which *narrows* the claim. The broadest claim is one that requires the least said about it. With claims, as with certain other matters in the field of human endeavor, the less said the better.

For example, the shortest and therefore broadest claim I am aware of is for an element, Californium, discovered by Glenn T. Seaborg and colleagues at the University of California at Berkeley (a little plug here for my *alma mater*). Claim 1 reads "Element 98". (You might think an *element* could not be patentable, but recall the transuranium elements are not naturally occurring so element 98 is man-made and thus patentable). Now that is a broad claim. Seaborg also discovered elements 94–102 and 106 including plutonium (94) and was awarded the Nobel Prize for Chemistry in 1951. His name will live on as he also got possibly the longest lasting award one can think of— element 106 was officially named Seaborgium in 1994.

The goal of a typical patent attorney is to cover the invention with as broad a claim as possible, usually claim 1. Then follows a number of more detailed claims, i.e., less broad claims until the last claim that is generally the narrowest. There is no law requiring this order so occasionally a broader claim may come later in the series.

There are generally two types of claims. One is called independent and the other is called dependent. The independent claim stands on its own while the dependent one refers to another claim. The dependent claim is a shorthand way of claiming a new element without reciting all the old elements again. For example claim 1 below is an independent claim followed by claim 2, a dependent claim:

1. A method for treating spasticity comprising administering to a spastic patient an effective amount of a botulinum toxin.
2. The method of claim 1 wherein the botulinum toxin is botulinum toxin Type A.

There are other forms of claims with names and much more could be said about them, but the take home on claims is that they *define the scope of the invention* and that is what a patent covers, no more and no less. When someone asks what does the patent cover, you must read the claims to find out.

5. What is Not Patentable?

(a) Laws of Nature

Ideas or principles or laws of nature are not patentable, as well as mathematical expressions and purely mental steps such as algorithms and computer programs, except when patented in combination with hardware. Recently, the courts have allowed so called "business method patents" such as the one click ordering of merchandise on the Internet which previously were denied as being purely mental steps. Cloning methods are patentable, but not cloned human beings, though genetically engineered bacteria and mice, among other living things, have been patented.

The famous Harvard mouse, altered to develop cancer, was the first patented mammal, (patented in the U.S. in 1988), but it still bothers some people that "life" can be patented. Recently, the European Patent Office finally upheld the corresponding European patent, which initially had been approved in 1992, against objections by church, environmental and animal protection groups, including Greenpeace, who had argued for cancellation on the grounds that it violated the dignity of living beings.

(b) Natural Substances

What about naturally occurring compounds in plants, frog skins or ocean sponges? The answer is that a naturally occurring compound may be patented if the discovery is in identifying and separating it in practical quantities if that had not been done before. I call that the "compound-in-a-bottle" test. If a naturally occurring compound or protein in the body did not previously exist in a bottle, you can probably patent it.

(c) Inherency

Also not patentable are inventions that are inherent e.g., the discovery of the actual mechanism of action of a drug for treatment of a given cancer when it was previously known to use the drug to treat the same cancer. The mechanism of action was inherent in the previous use of the drug and is therefore not separately patentable even though it was never known before. However, knowledge of such a mechanism could be used to discover a new compound to treat the same disease or a new use for the same cancer drug (e.g., for a new type of cancer or another disease) and that would not be inherent and so could be patentable. In short, discovering *why* something works may be good science, but it may not be patentable. A good example of this concerns the world's first synthetic drug.

(d) Story of Aspirin

The glycoside salicin, the bitter principle in willow leaves and bark, had been used for thousands of years as a folk remedy for treatment of pain, inflammation and fever. In the body, salicin is metabolized into salicylic acid, which was effective, but was hard on the stomach. This much was known on August 10, 1897 when Felix Hoffmann, a chemist at a German dyestuffs company called Bayer added an acetyl group to the salicylic acid molecule and came up with acetylsalicylic acid or aspirin. Arguably, this was the beginning of the modern drug era.

In more recent times, Sir John Vane, the British pharmacologist, was awarded a British Knighthood and the Nobel Prize for Medicine in 1982 for discovering the precise mechanism of action of *how* aspirin works through inhibition of certain enzymes that produced inflammatory compounds called prostaglandins. While the discovery was brilliant, it would not have been patentable as being inherent.

A discovery or invention may also not be patentable because it doesn't meet the basic requirements for patentability.

6. Requirements for Patentability

The rules are deceptively simple. Apart from the requirements for a proper written disclosure of the invention (a written description and an enabling disclosure), an invention must be:

- new or novel
- useful
- non-obvious and
- invented by the applicant for the patent.

(a) New or Novel

Something new or novel to a U.S. inventor means that no one patented or published the exact same invention anywhere in the world or used it or sold it or offered it for sale in the U.S. or had public knowledge of it more than a year before you made the invention. Outside the U.S., there is generally no so-called "grace period" of one year, though there are limited exceptions. Therefore, public disclosure of an invention by anyone including the inventor before filing for patent will generally act to invalidate the patent outside the U.S., unless the persons the invention was disclosed to were under a non-disclosure or secrecy agreement or the invention was being tested before completion. ("Testing" is a term that may be difficult to establish legally and so it can become a trap for the unwary.)

The publication date of an article is considered to be the date it became available to the public and not the date it was submitted for publication. Also, any public presentation, for example, at a scientific meeting, that discloses an invention acts as a bar to a patent on that invention outside of the U.S. if the patent has not been filed before the disclosure. However, the one year grace period would allow the patent to be obtained in the U.S. if a patent application were filed within a year of the disclosure.

(b) Useful

Just about any alleged use for an invention is sufficient to meet the legal obligation for an invention being useful, though it must have a "substantial utility" and provide a specific benefit in currently available form (*Brenner v. Manson*, U.S. Supreme Ct. 1966). A pharmaceutical patent will typically allege a number of possible medical uses for the invention and the patent is valid even if only a single use is ultimately found to be practical. In biotech, portions of genes involving simple sequences of amino acids known as "expressed sequence tags" or ESTs useful only for research have been rejected as not having met the legal requirement for being useful.

Some promising drug candidates have the opposite problem; too many uses or as I call it, "a drug in search of a disease". While they may have great potential for use as a drug for a variety of medical indications, they never become commercially useful for a single one. However, the usefulness required by the patent laws does not mean commercially useful or even FDA approvable, so that is not an issue for patenting such a compound.

(c) Non-obvious

This is almost always the main question concerning patentability. Typically, an invention is new and useful or no one would bother filing a patent on it. The law says non-obviousness must be viewed from the perspective of one of ordinary skill in the subject matter to which the invention pertains with knowledge of all prior public uses and publications relating to such subject matter, taken as a whole. The law of non-obviousness fills whole libraries so thankfully this book is not intended to go into it in any detail. However, that is what patent attorneys spend most of their time and your money on in trying to convince the Patent Examiners of the world's patent offices that the invention in front of them is not obvious.

In order to be rejected in the patent office on the grounds of non-obviousness (known in the trade as a "103" rejection after the U.S. code section, 35 USC 103, which defines non-obviousness), an Examiner may combine any number of prior art references that relate to your invention and reject your claims as being obvious in light of the combination. This is in contrast to a rejection for lack of novelty that requires that the prior art disclosure be in a single document.

So for example, if you were claiming the first metal tennis racquet, the Examiner could reject you by combining one reference showing a conventional wooden racquet with a second reference showing that it was known to replace wood with metal in other sports devices such as skis. That would establish what the Patent Office would call a "prima facie" case of obviousness or obvious on its face. In order to overcome this rejection, the inventor would have to submit further argument as to why it would not be obvious to substitute metal for wood in a tennis racquet or that by doing so, one obtained certain unexpected results such as superior accuracy or faster ball speed off the racquet or whatever. A finding of unexpected results typically overcomes the prima facie case of obviousness. That is why patent lawyers are always looking for *unexpected results* as it is often the key to obtaining a patent. (A friend of mine, a pilot, once told me that pilots were always looking for a place to land. I asked what about lawyers? He said lawyers were always looking for a situation in which a great deal of money was about to change hands!)

7. Inventorship

Concerning inventorship, the U.S. law provides that a patent may only be granted to the inventor(s) of the invention as defined by the claims. An inventor is one who first conceived the invention, where conception is defined as the formation in the mind of the inventor of a definite and permanent idea of the complete and operative invention. Someone who was involved in the invention may not be an inventor if that person played no part in conceiving the invention. This is different from authorship on a scientific paper where anyone who contributed to the paper can be an author.

With a patent, the inventors must be limited to those that conceived the invention which includes reducing it to practice if the reduction to practice included an inventive contribution to one or more of the claims. Thus one who conceives of using a drug for a new treatment might be a co-inventor with a doctor who discovered the necessary dosage forms or dose of the drug or treatment regimen to obtain the desired result. If the amounts and dosage form and treatment regimen used was conventional, then the doctor would not likely be a co-inventor, but merely one who assisted the inventor.

The reason that the correct inventors must be named on a patent is that having the wrong inventors may invalidate the patent, though if an innocent mistake is made without deceptive intent, inventorship can be corrected at any time. Outside the U.S., the issue of inventorship is not as important, as patents may be filed in the name of the assignee company for example. As a result, U.S. patent attorneys must identify the true and correct inventors for each patent application and not have too many or too few. Also, who is the first or last listed name on a scientific paper is important to scientists, but has no meaning in a patent.

8. Proof of Invention

Another urban legend about patents is that you have to be able to prove that your invention works before you can file a patent. While that sounds reasonable, it is not true. There is no requirement that you must have proof that your invention works before you file your patent application. You can hypothesize a plausible invention and file a patent application on it. That is because the law provides that the filing of a patent application is the legal equivalent to having completed the invention. (The legal way to say this is the filing of a patent application is a *constructive reduction to practice*).

You can also think up any number of pharmaceutical new use inventions and file patents on them. For example, if I conclude that floor wax can treat cancer based only on my belief that it can, I can file a patent application on that new use for floor wax with no data or proof of any kind that it treats cancer. This is a valid patent application and *if* a patent were granted on it, it would be a valid patent so long as the patent described in reasonable detail how to make and use the invention. But that does not really answer the question of whether such a patent in fact *would be* granted by a patent examiner.

If a patent examiner does not believe your invention is credible, he can ask for proof before granting it. If you have no proof, you will typically not obtain your patent. So, you say, you do need proof before you can get a patent. Well, the answer is sometimes you do and sometimes you don't, but it is still the case that you don't need proof *before you file* the patent application. Many worthwhile medical inventions are filed as patent applications long before there is any real clinical evidence that they work, though such proof may be forthcoming at a later time. And if the invention is explained in a credible way, proof may not be requested and the patent can properly be granted without proof. That is the beauty of the concept of "constructive reduction to practice".

Historically the practice of requiring proof to patent a drug actually started around the late 1800s and early 1900s when hucksters started patenting drug formulations and calling them *Patent Medicines*. These were mostly snake oil and other questionable nostrums for treating whatever ailed you and the Patent Office was being criticized for facilitating these scams by awarding patents. That was when the Patent Office started asking for proof of efficacy and denying patents for unproven remedies.

Take Home Message

- A patent is a sword, not a shield, has no defensive characteristics and gives you no rights other than the right for a limited time to exclude others.
- A patent generally expires 20 years from the date of its earliest effective filing date, or the longer of that date or 17 years from its issue date if filed in the U.S. before June 8, 1995.
- The life of one patent covering an approved pharmaceutical product may be extended by up to five years to make up for time lost in obtaining FDA approval for marketing.
- Patents are typically filed in one's home country first and then abroad within 12 months to maintain the benefit of the initial filing date.
- Use of the PCT can reserve your foreign rights for an additional 19 months.
- To understand a patent, you must first understand the claims. Claims define the scope of an invention, as a deed defines property.
- To be patentable, an invention must be new, useful, non-obvious and invented by the applicant.
- You do not need proof your invention works before you file a patent.

The next Chapter discusses **Patent Enforcement and Infringement**.

CHAPTER 2

Patent Enforcement and Infringement

1. Patent Enforcement

While the government grants a patent, it is up to the owner or exclusive licensee to enforce it in a court of law. The courts that have primary jurisdiction over patents in the U.S. are the Federal District Courts. These courts determine both validity and infringement of a patent at the same time. All appeals from a decision of one of the Federal District Courts are to a single appeals court, the Court of Appeals for the Federal Circuit in Washington, DC (CAFC). The only appeal from that Court is to the U.S. Supreme Court. This results in a certain consistency in the Federal District Courts, though as they say, your mileage may vary.

Outside the U.S., the court systems also vary and in some countries such as Japan and Germany, the civil courts decide infringement, but another specialized Patent Court or the Patent Office decides validity in a separate proceeding. As a result, one can sue an infringer and win a court case on infringement, but then the infringer can ask to have another court block the first court by holding the patent invalid. In the U.S. and U.K., the same court decides both validity and infringement at the same time so there is more finality. The Courts that decide validity in effect second guess the Patent Office and decide whether the patent should have been granted in the first place. In the U.S. and most other countries, a patent is presumed valid, which means the infringer has the burden of persuading the Court that the Patent Office was wrong in granting the patent.

2. Burden of Proof

In the U.S., the burden of proof in a patent validity case is greater than the typical burden of proof in a civil case which requires "a preponderance of the evidence", i.e., 51%, but less than the far more well known and stringent criminal standard of guilt "beyond a reasonable doubt". The validity standard is in-between the other standards and requires "clear and convincing evidence" of invalidity to overturn a patent. This is an important distinction as it means an infringer must provide very persuasive evidence of invalidity to a judge or jury in order to overturn a patent.

3. Trials in the U.S.

In the U.S., it is typical for patent cases to be tried before a jury, though they may be tried before a judge only. For example, cases involving generic challenges to branded drugs are generally tried before a judge. On the whole, juries seem to like patents and tend not to overturn them on grounds of lacking validity as they don't feel comfortable in revoking a patent that has been granted by the United States Patent Office. Patent infringement cases can be very expensive and legal fees often cost each side in the millions of dollars.

4. Trials outside the U.S.

Judges decide patent infringement cases outside the U.S. With the exception of the U.K., costs in European countries tend to be significantly less than in the U.S., though the combined costs of multiple infringement cases going on at the same time in several European countries add up. This is due to the fact that while one can file a single patent application with the European Patent Office (EPO) to cover all the European countries (27 at this time), the patent that results technically becomes a separate national patent in each country and each country retains jurisdiction over it in its courts for questions of infringement and validity. This allows the same patent to be held infringed in one European country by a given product and held not to be infringed by the same product in another and this has happened.

There have been numerous attempts to provide a true European-wide patent that could be enforced in a single European Court, but the individual countries have not been willing to give up their sovereignty on this issue to date and the specific issue of which language(s) would be controlling has also prevented implementation

5. Infringement

In order to infringe a patent, a product or process must incorporate each and every element of at least one of the claims of a patent. For example, if a patent claim covers four features or elements of a product, in order to infringe, the product would have to include each and every one of those four features or elements. It could have additional features or elements and still infringe, but it will not infringe if it does not contain all four.

Patents can be infringed either literally or by equivalents. Literal infringement means that the product or process incorporates each and every element of a single claim. For example, if I have a patent that claims a certain device consisting of five elements attached to a wall with a nail, you are a literal infringer if you manufacture, use or sell the same device containing the same elements attached to a wall by a nail. But what if you have the same device, etc... but it is attached to the wall with a screw? That is not literal infringement, but it might be infringement under the legal *doctrine of equivalents*.

The Courts developed the concept of infringement by equivalents to avoid the situation in which an insignificant or insubstantial change to a product or process would allow an infringer to get around a legitimate patent. In this case, the patent owner should have claimed a wall fastener and not a nail to insure literal infringement, but a court could decide that in the context of the invention, a screw was the *equivalent* of a nail and find the device infringed under the doctrine of equivalents.

Of course, nothing is simple and whole libraries are devoted to what is and what is not an equivalent. Unfortunately, while this doctrine is well intended, its effect creates a kind of *patent uncertainty principle*. That is, you would like to know if your gizmo infringes a certain patent. You ask a patent attorney and he may tell you it does not infringe the patent literally because you do not have one of the specifically claimed elements in your gizmo, but it might infringe under the doctrine of equivalents because your gizmo has an element that performs a similar function by similar means in a similar way as the claimed element that you did not have (like substituting the screw for the nail). That is not much comfort and is frustrating to patent owners and patent attorneys alike because it is difficult to be sure one way or the other. Anyway, that is the way the patent cookie crumbles, so we just have to live with the uncertainty until a court rules on the matter. However, in the meantime, you can get an opinion.

6. Infringement and Validity Opinions Generally

It is often the case that a company obtains an infringement and validity opinion on a patent if it is interested in enforcing it or if it is worried that the patent might be enforced against it. These opinions are performed by an in-house patent attorney or more generally by an outside patent attorney or firm. There is a second reason a possible infringer might obtain such an opinion and that is for legal protection against a claim of willful infringement. In a successful infringement case, the Court can award additional damages up to three times actual damages if the Court finds the infringer "willfully" infringed. A normal defense to such a claim of willfulness is having previously obtained an adequate opinion from an independent, competent counsel that the patent was invalid or not infringed and that the opinion was relied upon. In this way, the opinion shields the infringer from the claim that he acted willfully as he can claim he relied on the opinion.

This is also the point at which the management at a pharmaceutical company asks the patent attorney if the company patent in question is "*good*" and "*strong*". These are hard questions to answer literally because the person asking the question really wants to know if the company is going to win if they sue an infringer and assumes if the patent is good and strong it will. In fact, these adjectives are somewhat contradictory in patent parlance. "Good" would presumably mean the patent broadly claims the subject matter and thereby provides good protection against infringers. "Strong" would mean the patent was defensible in court and that usually requires the claims to be narrow in scope so as to be defensible against attacks on validity. A broad patent is much more likely to be successfully attacked on grounds of invalidity than a narrow patent. Nonetheless the patent attorney knows that the real question behind the question asked is "*will we win the case?*" and he answers accordingly.

If counsel cautions against litigation because of some possible problems with enforcing a patent, he often hears from management something like "well then why did we get the blasted patent in the first place if we can't sue on it!" The answer is that patents have a variety of uses, only one of which is marching into court. These include licensing, cross-licensing, being part of the IP assets of a company that are important in assessing overall value of the enterprise, and my favorite, the "standoff", where each side claims to have one or more patents covering the other side's products and both say "if you sue me, I'll sue you". In addition, multiple patents relating to your own products and potential improvements have a cumulative defensive effect and act to discourage investment by competitors in areas close to those you have patented.

Regarding patent strategies, one of the best is to try to patent your competitors' products. This seems odd since it would seem you should be patenting your own products. But this strategy flows naturally from the nature of a patent right that is only to exclude others. For example, you might be the first to discover acrylic polymers have advantages over other classes of polymers used for making intraocular lenses used to replace cataracts. Your competitor in that field may be secretly working on his own new lens with his own acrylic polymer different from the polymer in your new lens, but if his polymer falls within the scope of your broad patent covering the use of any acrylic polymer for making intraocular lenses, you have, in effect, patented his future product even though you did not know what it was. That means *the best patent defense is patent offence.* So when a competitor comes threatening with a patent covering one of your important products, you reply confidently that you have a patent covering one of their really important products and they can pound sand.

7. Infringement Opinions

In the case of an infringement opinion, the attorney compares the potentially infringing product or process with the claims of the patent to determine if the claims cover the product or process. In order to do this, the attorney must read the patent and review the file history of the patent to determine the scope of the claims, i.e., what the claims cover and what they do not cover literally and by the aforementioned doctrine of equivalents. That is because the file history of the patent includes the patent prosecution before the Patent Office that typically consists of written rejections by patent examiners and written replies by patent attorneys giving reasons why the examiner incorrectly rejected the claims presented for examination.

In the U.S., statements made by inventors or their attorneys during patent prosecution are taken into consideration in defining the breadth or meaning of the claims. So if during prosecution of the patent, an attorney makes a statement as to what a patent claim is intended to cover and what it does not cover, the patent owner cannot later say in an infringement case that his claim covers something his attorney gave up earlier during prosecution to obtain the patent. This is called *prosecution history estoppel* if you really wanted to know.

As a result, patent attorneys have to be very careful about what they write to the Patent Office and that leads to the practice of asking for personal interviews with the Examiner rather than putting forth arguments in writing. After the interview, the Examiner or attorney may write a few lines about what was said for the record, but that usually does not result in any significant problems for the patent owner.

Interestingly, most of the rest of the world's courts don't seem to care very much about what was said in obtaining the patent in their country's patent offices and the courts decide what a patent covers, i.e., the scope of the claims, independently of what was said to obtain it.

8. Validity Opinions

In the case of a validity opinion, the attorney reviews the patent and the prior art references (prior patents or publications related to the invention) cited by the Patent Office and the inventor and will likely conduct

an independent search for additional prior art references to see if there are any disclosures of the invention or offers of sale more than one year before the
patent application was filed which could invalidate it.
The purpose is to try to find anything that would cast
doubt on the validity of the patent. Of course, the possible infringer's attorney is looking for evidence that the
patent is invalid, while the patent owner wants to avoid
surprise and determine the strength of his case.

9. Damages

If a Court finds a party has infringed a valid and
enforceable drug patent, the Court awards damages
for the infringement and generally issues a permanent
injunction barring the infringer from making the drug
product until the patent expires. In the U.S., damages
take the form of either lost profits or a reasonable royalty. Attorney's fees are also awarded in exceptional
cases such as willful infringement or bad faith litigation. Outside the U.S., the loser pays a substantial portion of the winner's attorney's fees in every patent case.
Damages in the U.S. can be very large, sometimes
hundreds of millions of dollars, though typically smaller awards are made. In Hatch Waxman cases, only
injunctions may be granted and no damages are
awarded, though attorney's fees may be granted in an
exceptional case to either winning side.

Take Home Message

- In the U.S., patents are enforced in the Federal
  Courts, often in a jury trial.
- A patent is presumed valid and an infringer has
  the burden of proof to overturn a patent.
- Damages for infringement are either lost profits
  or a reasonable royalty.
- A product or process can infringe literally or
  under the doctrine of equivalents.

- To infringe a patent, the infringing product or process must incorporate each and every element of at least one claim in a patent.
- One accused of infringement often obtains an infringement or validity opinion to rely on as a defense against additional damages for infringing willfully.

The next chapter discusses **Pharmaceutical, Biological and Medical Device Patents** .

CHAPTER 3

Pharmaceutical, Biological and Medical Device Patents

1. Pharmaceutical Patents Generally

Pharmaceutical patents are generally no different than other patents, except that under current U.S. law, a generic manufacturer can obtain the right to copy an innovative drug under certain circumstances if there is no valid patent covering it. This puts the onus on innovative drug manufacturers to protect their investment in the development and registration of their innovative drugs by obtaining and maintaining as many patents as they can that cover them. Typical pharmaceutical patents cover active drug compounds, their intermediates, metabolites, hydrates, salts and esters; combinations with other active drugs; methods of manufacturing the active drug and its intermediates; different methods of medical treatment using the drugs including novel indications and dosage regimens; formulations for the drug including new dosage forms; devices containing the drugs such as skin patches, drug delivery systems, etc...

2. Hierarchy of Patents

(a) Compound Patents

The best pharmaceutical patent is a compound patent. This type of patent claims the active drug compound as well as its salts, esters and hydrates. It also typically covers a broad range of similar compounds to prevent a competitor from making a chemically similar drug. One common strategy is to file a broad patent on the compound, and then file a continuing application narrowly covering the active drug agent that is expected to become the approved product. This will result in the granting of two patents with the same expiration date both covering the approved product. The first one will be "good" as it is broad and the second will be "strong" as it is narrow.

The reason the compound patent is the best pharmaceutical patent is that it covers a drug product no matter how it is formulated, no matter how it is made, no matter what it is sold for and no matter what use it is put to, as long as it contains the patented compound. According to a recent Court of Appeals (CAFC) decision which overturned a lower court ruling on this issue (*SmithKline v. Apotex*, CAFC 2004), even the *amount* of that compound is not important, so that a drug product will infringe a compound patent even if it contains only a trace of the patented compound and even if an infringer did his best to try to keep that trace out of his product.

(b) Medical Use Patents

The next most valuable type of pharmaceutical patent is a medical use patent. This type of patent covers the approved medical use or indication of an approved drug product. It can also cover unapproved medical uses. Typically, a medical use claim for treatment of a specific disease or condition is directly infringed only by a patient with that disease or condition or by the doctor for prescribing it, but not by the drug product manufacturer. However, the law makes one that actively induces another to infringe liable as a direct infringer. When a drug product is put on the market, it must contain instructions for use and these instructions provide the necessary "active inducement" to charge the manufacturer with infringement. As a result, a medical use patent will effectively prevent infringement of a drug product labeled for the patented use.

What about infringement of off-label patents, that is, patents which cover a medical use *not* on the label of a drug product, since many drugs today are used extensively by doctors for off-label medical uses? That is a more difficult question to answer and that is one reason why a compound patent is better than a use patent, since there is infringement with a compound patent regardless of the use.

There are two general situations in which off-label infringement occurs. The first is off-label use where an infringing product is labeled and sold for a given use, but prescribed by physicians for a patented use not on the FDA approved label. In order to show inducement of infringement, the patent owner would have to provide evidence that the drug manufacturer knew of the off-label use and actively induced others to infringe. This tends to be an issue that revolves around obtaining evidence of knowledge and intent of the drug manufacturer including evidence of any overt acts to induce infringement. Examples of activities that could suggest active inducement are any promotional or informational activities for the off-label use by the manufacturer or by third parties connected to the manufacturer in one way or another, such as statements by company sales people, company website references to the indication or educational programs for physicians to teach the off-label use that are directly or indirectly sponsored by the manufacturer.

The second off-label use is in the context of an ANDA filing for a generic drug. Until recently, it was common practice for innovators to list off-label patents in the FDA Orange Book which would then require generic companies to file Paragraph IV certifications which would allow the patent holder/innovator to file

suit against the generic company for patent infringement and would prevent the FDA from approving the
generic drug for 30 months. The current case law
(*Warner-Lambert v. Apotex*, CAFC 2003) and related
FDA regulations and recent legislation make it clear
that innovators can no longer list off-label patents in
the Orange Book. This is discussed in more detail in
future chapters.

However, where a generic company tries to obtain
labeling for less than all the approved uses for an innovative drug, and one of those uses is patented by the
innovator, the innovator may still sue for infringement.
In a recent case, (*Takeda v. Watson Pharmaceuticals,
2003*), a lower court ruled a patent holder may sue a
generic company for inducing infringement of its use
patent based on the filing of an ANDA even though the
application was pending and no sales had been made.

(c) Formulation Patents

The third basic type of patent for drug products is a
formulation patent that typically covers the active
drug agent in the specific formulation for use in the
body. Sometimes, the formulation patent covers a
unique excipient such as a stabilizer or preservative
used in the formulation. A formulation patent offers the
least desirable patent protection because typically it can
be avoided by using a different formulation. However, in
the context of an ANDA submission for a generic drug,
a formulation patent, no matter how narrow, may be
ideally suited to prevent copying of the drug by a generic company.

This is because of the regulatory requirements for
pharmaceutical equivalence and bioequivalence that a
generic drug must meet. While a generic drug is
allowed to have minor changes in the formulation or
even in the active drug agent, typically that would
require clinical trials to establish bioequivalence since
the generic drug and the reference drug would not be

"the same". To avoid the expense and time of clinical trials, most generic companies simply copy the innovator's drug formulation exactly and try to invalidate the formulation patent. In this way, even a very narrow formulation patent can be extremely valuable in preventing generic copying, even though it would be easy to get around the patent by reformulating. Patent attorneys should not forget to obtain very narrow formulation claims covering an innovator product in addition to broad ones, as narrow formulation claims are easier to defend against attacks on validity.

3. Biologicals Patents

Biotechnology patents are not different in principle from pharmaceutical patents except that they use "bio-speak" and claim recombinant genes, proteins, monoclonal antibodies, nucleic acids and DNA sequences and their methods of manufacture, instead of the smaller molecules of chemically based pharmaceutical products. Biologicals are generally defined by their method of manufacture. That is, a biological is manufactured by a biological process rather than by a chemical process, as are conventional pharmaceuticals. However, for FDA purposes, even though antibiotics are often produced by a biological process such as fermentation, they are thought of as conventional drugs and they are handled by FDA administratively as drugs rather than biologicals, while all recombinant products, vaccines, toxins, allergens and all blood related products are handled administratively as biologicals regardless how they are made.

4. Medical Device Patents

Typical medical device patents cover stents, intraocular lenses, heart-lung machines, etc...and they follow the same basic principles for patents in general.

The big difference between patents for biologicals and medical devices, and patents for pharmaceuticals is that only the latter may be listed in the FDA Orange Book and come within the scope of the Hatch Waxman Act. As a result, biologicals and medical devices may not be genericized as pharmaceuticals. However, there are regulatory procedures for medical devices that allow them to be accepted based on similarity to an approved medical device and that is discussed in more detail in the next chapter. The future likelihood of generic biologicals is also discussed at the end of Chapter 7.

Take Home Message

- There are three basic types of pharmaceutical patents: compound, method of use and formulation.
- Compound patents provide the best protection for a drug product because they are broad.
- Method of use patents typically provide intermediate protection, especially for approved medical use claims.
- Formulation patents generally provide the least protection, but may still provide good protection against a generic product that copies the patented formulation, because infringement is clear from copying and a narrow patent is often more defensible (i.e., the patent is "strong") than a broader one.

The previous three chapters have discussed patents, the first leg of the three-legged stool of product life-cycle management. The next two chapters discuss the second regulatory leg: **U.S. Food and Drug Administration** and related **Drug Product Exclusivity**.

CHAPTER 4

Overview of FDA

1. FDA Generally

The U.S. Food and Drug Administration or FDA is a governmental agency charged with insuring that the nation's food supply is unadulterated and medicines and medical devices are safe and effective. Generally speaking, in order to market a new or generic drug or Class III medical device or biological in the U.S., one must first obtain pre-market approval from the FDA. Over-the-counter non-prescription medicines such as, for example, headache and cough/cold medicines are regulated by monograph, which means the FDA establishes written guidelines for these products and if you meet the guidelines, you can sell the product.

Products containing herbs and other natural ingredients that do not make medical use label claims generally do not require pre-market approval under current law. If the FDA has evidence that they are unsafe, the FDA can remove them from the market. The most recent case in point is ephedrine-containing OTC products. This is in contrast to drugs and medical devices that must prove their safety and efficacy before marketing is permitted.

Other countries have similar agencies regulating drugs sold in that country. Approval by one major country does not provide approval in another, though some of the smaller countries will accept a drug for sale in its country if it is approved by a major country's health agency under what was called a Certificate of

Free Sale, now called a Certificate of Pharmaceutical Product. In addition, there are regional approval systems such as the EMEA in Europe where approval by that agency allows marketing in many of the countries of Europe. However, generally, one must satisfy each major country's FDA equivalent Ministry of Health in order to market a drug product in that country.

2. Origins of FDA

The modern FDA began in 1906 with the passage of the Federal Food and Drug Act. Prior to that time, the states had primary control over food and drugs. The 1906 Act was the result of a national furor over improper conditions in the meatpacking industry that Upton Sinclair wrote about in *The Jungle*. This began a pattern for the next century where new laws regulating food and drugs were enacted in response to terrible conditions or accidents. The 1906 law had no pre-market approval aspects and drugs were required to be in accordance with the standards of strength, quality and purity set out in the *United States Pharmacopoeia*.

In 1939, a Tennessee company marketed a form of an anti-infective sulfa drug for children called Elixir Sulfanilamide. Unfortunately, it was formulated with an alcohol related to antifreeze and never tested before marketing. Over 100 people died, many of whom were children. Public outcry again provided the impetus for a new law to regulate drugs, cosmetics and medical devices. It required that drugs be labeled with adequate directions for use, mandated safety to be established, prohibited false therapeutic claims and authorized factory inspections.

In response to the thalidomide disaster (thalidomide was a sedative that was approved and sold in Europe, but had not yet been approved for sale in the U.S.) which produced thousands of deformed newborns outside the U.S., the law was amended in 1962 to require that both safety and efficacy had to be established before a drug could be approved and sold in the U.S. It also added stricter controls over clinical trials and established acceptable manufacturing practices for the drug industry and provided FDA additional powers to inspect manufacturing facilities. In addition, the new law required all antibiotics to be certified and gave FDA control of prescription drug advertising. As an interesting historical footnote, thalidomide was recently approved by the FDA to treat leprosy and is being used off-label for treatment of cancer.

Medical devices came under additional scrutiny in 1976 as the result of injuries to thousands of women caused by the Dalcon Shield intrauterine device (IUD). Thereafter, medical devices were subjected to more rigorous regulatory control.

In 1983, the Orphan Drug Act became law and was designed to promote development of products for rare diseases, defined as diseases with less than 200,000 patients in the U.S. The law provides a seven-year marketing exclusivity and a 50% tax credit for research expenses.

Also in 1983, the Bureau of Drugs merged with the Bureau of Biologics to form the National Center for Drugs and Biologics (NCDB). In 1987, they were split into two divisions: the Center for Drug Evaluation and Research (CDER pronounced "see-der") and the Center for Biologics Evaluation and Research (CBER pronounced "see-ber"). Recently, they are in the process of coming closer together again administratively.

(a) PDMA and PDUFA

In 1988, the Prescription Drug Marketing Act (PDMA) became law. In 1992, the Generic Drug Enforcement Act came into being and the Office of Generic Drugs (OGD) was formed as part of FDA. The OGD continues to have responsibility for approval of generic drugs.

Also in 1992, the Prescription Drug User Fee Act (PDUFA pronounced "puh-doofa") required drug and biologic manufacturers to pay fees to FDA for the evaluation of NDAs and BLAs, currently $573,500 per filing. A 1997 amendment provided that small businesses got a break and owed no fee for their first filing of an NDA. If the filing is for a bioequivalence study only, the fee is cut in half. The user fees were intended to allow the hiring of more reviewers and thus speed new drug approvals. Against expectations, this has actually had its intended effect and the number of new drug approvals has increased, with the median time to approval cut in half from two years to one year.

A phrase you will hear from time to time is the PDUFA date. That is the date the FDA is required by PDUFA to complete its review of an NDA and it is generally ten months following acceptance of the NDA by FDA. The FDA can reject or approve an NDA at that time, but if FDA does not approve the NDA, it typically sends an "approvable letter" which indicates what additional information the FDA requires to approve it. PDUFA also requires FDA to set out all of its requirements for approval on the PDUFA date and it may not sandbag, i.e., add new requirements in the future, unless there are special circumstances.

(b) Biologicals

Technically, biologicals are regulated under the Public Health Services Act of 1902 which provided pre-marketing approval originally for therapeutic agents of biological origin such as vaccines and now of greater interest, biotech products. That means that drugs and biologicals are not regulated under the same statute. However, by and large, BLAs are evaluated in the same manner as NDAs and the applicant must similarly establish safety and efficacy before its BLA will be approved. One result of this difference is that while there are numerous generics of drugs, there are currently no generic biological products because technically the Public Health Services Act does not provide for them, while the drug act does. The potential for future generics of biologicals is discussed at the end of Chapter 7.

(c) DDMAC

FDA through its division called DDMAC, which stands for "Division of Drug Marketing, Advertising and Communications" (but no one can remember its name so it is universally referred to as "DeeDeeMac") also reviews all promotional materials after approval and issues warning letters to industry that number in the thousands annually. DDMAC is the one that requires all the side effects warnings in TV ads and magazines that advertise drugs.

(d) FDAMA

Recent developments include the Food and Drug Administration Modernization Act of 1997 (FDAMA pronounced "fa-dahma", rhymes with "pajama"). This new law provides for pediatric exclusivity periods (more on that later) and provides for dissemination of so-called off-label information from peer-reviewed journals. Generally speaking, a drug company is forbidden to promote a drug for any unapproved indication or off-label use. However, a doctor is legally allowed to use an approved drug to treat a patient for any indication he or she believes appropriate. Many drugs have significant off-label uses and that results in a conundrum for the drug companies and doctors.

(e) Washington Legal Foundation

The FDA insisted the drug companies could not say *anything* about off-label uses including how to safely use its drugs for these off-label uses. This was a problem because doctors were using the drugs for off-label uses and the companies had no way of communicating to the doctor to insure that the drugs were being used safely. A foundation called the Washington Legal Foundation or WLF sued FDA on the grounds that this violated the first amendment of the U.S. constitution by forbidding commercial speech. Court decisions favored the WLF view and as a result, the companies are now allowed to provide copies of peer-reviewed medical and scientific journal articles showing the results of clinical trials on off-label uses to doctors that request such information.

3. Drug Industry Regulation

The FDA regulates the drug industry by requiring companies to obtain approval for major steps in the development of a drug and to establish that the drug is safe and effective for its intended use. In addition, the FDA oversees drug manufacturing and testing through the promulgation of lengthy and detailed written guidelines and procedures known as "Good Manufacturing Practices" or *GMPs* and "Good Laboratory Practices" or *GLPs*. Current GMPs or GLPs are known as cGMPs and cGLPs.

Drug development is done in two broad phases known as pre-clinical and clinical. In pre-clinical development, the drug is tested in animals to establish safety. In clinical development, the drug is tested in humans to establish safety and efficacy.

(a) Clinical Development: INDs and Phases I-IV

Clinical development is further broken down into five basic categories:

- Investigational New Drug (IND)
- Phase I
- Phase II
- Phase III and
- Phase IV testing.

The IND requires the sponsor to file for approval to start human testing. Phase I is testing in a small number of human volunteers for safety. Phase II is testing in a relatively small group of human volunteers with the disease or condition being treated for initial efficacy and for establishing the proper dose for the intended use of a new drug. Phase III is testing in a large number of patients having the disease or condition for both safety and efficacy. Phase IV is post marketing studies approved by FDA to monitor long-term safety. The number of patients required varies with the use or indication for which the drug is being tested. That is, the number of patients in a Phase III study is selected to establish efficacy statistically and may vary from a few hundred to tens of thousands.

(b) Well-controlled Studies

The FDA generally requires a minimum of two separate well-controlled Phase III studies in order to approve a new drug for market. A well-controlled study typically requires a double-masked, placebo controlled study in which some patients receive drug and some receive a non-drug-containing imitation or placebo and neither the patient nor the doctor know which patient is receiving the drug and which patient is receiving the placebo. In order to obtain approval for a new drug, both studies must be clinically relevant and demonstrate that the drug is safe and statistically more efficacious than the placebo.

4. Types of Drug Filings

New drugs are typically filed as a New Drug Application or NDA and generic drugs are filed as an Abbreviated New Drug Application or ANDA. Generic drugs may also be filed as a so-called "paper NDA" under a section of the regulations known as 505(b)(2) in which the branded drug formulation is modified in some minor way. Biologicals, that is, products that are derived from biological processes and which may use molecular biology or gene splicing, such as certain toxins and biotech products, are filed as a Biological License Application or BLA and have separate regulations and approval standards.

Recall that one very important distinction between NDAs and BLAs is there are no current regulations that allow generics or ANDAs to be filed for drugs approved as BLAs. However, recently the FDA has indicated that it is moving in that direction for certain older proteins such as recombinant human insulin and human growth hormone that were historically approved as NDAs and there has been pressure from generic trade groups and others to allow generics of all biotech products.

The usual reason stated for not allowing generics of biologicals is the inherent variability of biological processes used to manufacture complicated proteins, antibodies and the like as opposed to the more reproducible chemical processes used to manufacture a typical new drug made from a small molecule. Regardless of the reason, the fact that BLAs are currently protected from generics gives them an enormously beneficial status and allows their manufacturers to maintain market share for many years longer than a conventional new drug approved as an NDA.

5. Medical Devices

FDA also regulates medical devices as outlined in the Code of Federal regulations (21 CFR 800). Medical devices are divided into three classes. Class I relates to simple medical devices which present minimal potential for harm to the user, such as tongue depressors. Class III relates to devices that sustain or support life or are implanted, such as heart valves. Class II medical devices are those that fall in-between such as home pregnancy kits.

Class I devices require no testing, but are subject to general controls such as meeting GMPs. Class II devices are also subject to general controls and also "special controls" such as performance standards, post market surveillance and other regulations. Class III devices are the most regulated and require one of two forms of pre-market approval: a Premarket Notification (PMN, also known as the section 510K process) or a Pre-market Approval (PMA). Class III devices can only use the PMN process if the manufacturer can establish that its device is "substantially similar" to an earlier device that was marketed before 1976. As a result, new Class III devices must be filed as PMAs and require proof of safety and efficacy, much as a new drug. The initial FDA filing for a Class III device is called an IDE or Investigational Device Exemption that allows human testing much as an IND allows human testing for drugs. Under the applicable statute, FDA has six months to review a PMA after it is filed. The FDA also may require the manufacturer to comply with certain post-approval obligations.

Under the PMN process, the FDA may allow subsequent manufacturers to file a submission under section 510K of the regulations for Class II devices. If they can establish their product is "substantially similar" to the approved medical device, they can obtain "clearance" by the FDA to market their device. The "clearance" is not technically an approval, so those companies cannot say that they are "FDA approved". Nonetheless, the 510K clearance is a convenient and much less expensive shortcut to marketing a Class II device since no data on safety and efficacy is required.

6. Drug Agencies Outside the U.S.

(a) Europe

In Europe, there is the European Agency for Evaluation of Medicinal Products recently renamed the European Medicines Agency. While they changed the name, they left the acronym the same (EMEA). The EMEA uses a so-called "centralized procedure" in which there is a single review by all countries at one time and the approval is for all countries or none. The NDA there is called an MAA or Marketing Authorization Application. There is also another procedure called the MRP or Mutual Recognition Procedure in which you start with one country known as the RMS or Reference Member State. When the RMS approves your product, you can move on to other countries, called CMS or "Concerned Member States", to get their approvals. I mention these details just to give you a flavor of what appears to be bureaucracy gone wild. One almost expects to run across a specialized veterinary agency called AEROUS (with apologies to the movie *The Princess Bride*) short for Agency for Evaluation of Rodents Of Unusual Size.

The EMEA is also responsible for managing parallel imports of pharmaceutical products from one country in Europe to another. This is known as parallel trade. The way this works, for example, is when a company sells its drug product in Spain, a low priced country for drugs, the drugs are re-imported by third parties back to the higher priced European countries and sold again at higher prices, similar in principle to the proposed re-importation of U.S. drug products from Canada to the U.S. In the European Union or EU, (formerly known as the European Community or EC), a union of 25 European countries, patents will not prevent this on the theory of exhaustion of patent rights and the free movement of goods throughout the EU. That is, once a patented drug product is sold inside the EU, its patent rights are lost and may not be used to prevent re-importation to another member country of the EU, so long as the patent owner or one in concert with him made the first sale.

There is one exception to this rule which applies to the 10 new, mostly Eastern European countries that joined the EU on May 1, 2004 including Poland, the Czech Republic, Slovenia, Slovakia, Hungary, etc... For these countries, if the patent owner could not have obtained a patent in one of those countries due to the fact that pharmaceutical products were not patentable at the time of filing of the patents for the product in Europe, then parallel imports from that country are not allowed.

Pharmaceutical companies in Europe have tried to fight parallel trade, but with limited success. It is a form of generic competition, but with insult added to injury in that the parallel importers are selling *your own product* in competition with you. Some companies instituted programs to limit sales of products to those distributors who cooperated with parallel importers and the EU took the position that this was illegal anti-competitive behavior.

One company, Bayer, took the case to the top court in Europe, the European Court of Justice, and recently won. The court ruled that so long as Bayer acted unilaterally, and not under an agreement with anyone else, it could legally restrict and control sales of its own products as it wished. That has given pharmaceutical companies in Europe something to work with, but parallel imports continue to be problems for them since prices for the same products vary by country based partially on differing governmental pricing requirements, but also on significant differences in the cost of living in member counties.

(b) Japan

The Japan Health Ministry is called the Ministry of Health, Labor and Welfare (MHLW). The equivalent of their FDA was recently reorganized as of April 1, 2004 and now is called the Pharmaceutical and Medical Devices Agency (PMDA). It combined three previous agencies responsible for assessment and approval of drugs and medical devices into one agency, including KIKO, the one responsible for advising on clinical trials. The staff of the PMDA is substantially smaller than its counterparts in Europe and the U.S. and that in part accounts for the added time to approval. The PMDA is expected to double the current user fee charges to U.S. $150,000, about one quarter of the corresponding U.S. user fee. Average time for approval in Japan was 32 months in 1996, though that supposedly has been improved to 21 months in 2004, but that is still substantially longer than the average 12 months for approval in the U.S. and 16 months in Europe.

Japan has an interesting approach to minimizing issues about generics. When a drug is approved, it is assigned a reimbursement price by another government agency (the NHI price) and the government reimburses patients for the drug based on that price. The initial price of the drug tends to be high by U.S. standards. But every two years, the government lowers the NHI price on the majority of prescription drugs. For 2002, the average price reduction for 80% of drugs was 6.3%. For 2004, it was 4.2%. Over the normal lifetime of a drug, the NHI price of the drug drops significantly and by the time the patents and any regulatory exclusivity have expired, the price is already so low there is not much incentive for generics to enter the market. This constant price reduction is taking its toll on the health of the Japanese pharmaceutical industry and consolidation of companies in Japan, which has just recently started, will soon be the order of the day.

One other recent change of interest is the Pharmaceuticals Affairs Law that was amended in

2002 to add "distribution approval" to "manufacturing approval". This means a company will be able to seek approval of a drug without having to have its own manufacturing plant in Japan and will now be able to use contract manufacture for the approved product which was not allowed before. Also to be added is the system of using drug master files or DMFs to protect the intellectual property of bulk drug manufacturers, as is common in the U.S.

7. FDA Orange Book

The FDA Orange Book is the name used to describe an FDA publication "Approved Drug Products and Therapeutic Equivalents" available on line at **www.fda.gov/cder/ob**. The Orange Book is the place where the FDA lists all approved drugs, their dates of approval, for what indication or use they have been approved and the dates and types of regulatory exclusivities that apply to those drugs. The law also requires the patent owner or drug approval owner to list certain types of patents that cover the approved drug in the Orange Book. The patent listings in the Orange Book trigger portions of the Hatch Waxman Act that is covered in detail in Chapter 6. It was originally called the Orange Book because years ago it was only available as a hard copy bound in an orange cover. Now it is a website, but the name has stuck. As a tip of the hat to the old name, the entry page of the FDA Orange Book website is colored orange.

Currently, the types of patents that must be listed in the Orange Book are patents that claim the active drug in the drug product, the formulation of the drug product, an inactive ingredient or excipient present in the formulation or patents covering its approved indication or other conditions of use.

Patents relating to methods of manufacturing the active drug in the drug product may not be listed, but patents claiming novel active drug products claimed in product-by-process claims can be listed. (A product-by-process claim is one that claims a product by defining it in terms of the process by which it is made). Patents claiming metabolites of the active drug (i.e., compounds which are formed in the body by metabolic processes after the drug has been administered) or intermediates used in the manufacture of the active drug may not be listed. Packaging and container patents may not be listed. Patents claiming unapproved indications or uses may not be listed.

Patents for polymorphs (different physical forms of the active drug such as crystalline forms, waters of hydration, solvates and amorphous forms) that claim the same physical form as the approved drug product may be listed. However, polymorphs that contain a different physical form from the approved product may be listed only if the patent holder has data to demonstrate that the different polymorph is the "same" active substance (i.e. both pharmaceutically equivalent and bioequivalent) as the approved active drug.

The applicable statute requires that patents must be listed within 30 days of FDA approval of the drug product. If the patent is granted after approval of the drug product, it must be listed within 30 days of the patent grant. However, FDA regulations allow the FDA to list a patent submitted after this 30-day period, but an ANDA or paper NDA filed prior to the date of the late listing is not required to file a Paragraph IV certification for that late-listed patent. The patent owner may still sue the generic company on that patent, but the patentee is not entitled to a thirty-month stay for it. However, if there were one or more timely listed patents in the Orange Book, the patent owner would already have a 30-month stay in place, so he could simply add the new patent to the existing suit.

The basic purpose of the Orange Book is to list patents and FDA exclusivities for approved products. If a patent is listed in the Orange Book, a generic is required to provide a patent certification as part of its ANDA. The patent certification is a key element of the Hatch Waxman Act that is discussed in more detail in Chapter 6.

Take Home Message

- The FDA regulates the U.S. drug industry. In Europe, its counterpart is called the EMEA and in Japan, the PMDA.
- Clinical drug development consists of five phases: IND and Phases I-IV, all of which are closely monitored by FDA.
- New drugs are filed as NDAs, generic drugs are filed as ANDAs, biologicals are filed as BLAs and devices are filed as PMAs or 510Ks.
- The FDA Orange Book is where patents for approved drugs are listed as well as dates of any marketing or data exclusivity.
- ANDA and 505(b)(2) filers are required to file a patent certification if the Orange Book lists a patent covering the innovative product being copied at the time of filing the ANDA or 505(b)(2).

The next Chapter discusses **Drug Product Exclusivity**.

CHAPTER 5

Drug Product Exclusivity

1. Exclusivity of Drug Products Generally

Drug products have a number of different ways to obtain and maintain exclusivity. In this context, exclusivity means that the manufacturer retains exclusive rights to his drug product and no third party is entitled to copy it and thereby take market share through reduced prices. The basic exclusivities available are patent and regulatory and to a lesser extent trademarks and trade dress.

2. Patent Exclusivity

The most obvious exclusivity is by way of patents. A drug manufacturer will try to obtain one or more patents on the new chemical entity or NCE, and close relatives of it such as its salts, esters, polymorphs such as hydrates and isomers and other chemical forms of an NCE, alternative methods of manufacture, its formulation as an oral, topical or parenteral drug product, its use to treat a disease or condition, novel dosage forms or dosage regimens, combinations with other active drugs, new uses of treatment, etc... Patents can be obtained throughout the life of an active drug and used to help maintain exclusivity. Patents on new combinations, new uses and improved formulations are especially useful for this purpose.

3. Regulatory Exclusivity

There are six basic regulatory exclusivities available under current U.S. law and regulations. They are:

- new chemical entity or NCE exclusivity,
- new use or indication exclusivity,
- new formulation exclusivity,
- orphan drug exclusivity,
- pediatric exclusivity and
- 180-day generic product exclusivity for the "first-filer" generic company.

The following are the six exclusivities from longest to shortest.

(a) Orphan Drug Exclusivity

The "orphan" drug exclusivity is for seven years marketing exclusivity and prevents the FDA from approving a third party NDA or BLA (Biological License Application) as well as an ANDA (or paper NDA) for the same active drug or biologic for the same orphan indication during the seven year period. In short, the orphan drug exclusivity blocks approval of applications for the same active drug for the same medical indication. A second product may be approved if it uses a different drug chemically or if it is clinically superior, offers greater safety or is a major contribution to patient care.

To be eligible for orphan drug exclusivity, the drug product must be designated as an orphan drug by the FDA on the grounds that it is unprofitable or that it is for a disease or condition that affects less than 200,000 people in the U.S. and it must be the first designated drug to be approved for the orphan indication. Note that there is no restriction on *filing* an NDA or ANDA for an orphan drug before the seven- year period expires in contrast to the rule for NCE exclusivity.

Companies have used the Orphan Drug exclusivity as part of an overall plan to get an initial indication approved for the drug with future plans to extend the label indications. This is common for cancer drugs since the FDA requires proof of safety and efficacy for each type of cancer and oncologists commonly use cancer drugs off-label for other cancers.

(b) New Chemical Entity (NCE) Exclusivity

The law provides five years of marketing as well as data exclusivity in the U.S. from the date of approval of a drug containing an NCE. The five-year marketing exclusivity means that FDA will not approve an ANDA (or comparable paper NDA filed under 505(b)(2)) containing the same NCE for the same approved use for five years from the date of approval. The FDA may however approve an NDA for the same drug product.

In addition, the five year data exclusivity means that the FDA will not accept an ANDA (or paper NDA) filing until the end of the fifth year, unless a patent is listed in the FDA "Orange Book", and in such case the FDA will accept such a filing one year earlier, i.e., at any time after the end of the fourth year from marketing approval. This is highly significant as the mean time for approval of an ANDA is about 18 months, giving an effective marketing exclusivity typically longer than the five years.

The five-year exclusivity applies only to the first approval of an NCE in any drug product in the U.S. That is, if a second drug product for another use or indication containing that same NCE is filed by the same or different manufacturer, there is no second five year exclusivity allowed, even if the first drug product has been withdrawn or was never sold or the second drug product is in a completely different form for a completely different use as long as the first drug product was approved.

(c) New Use or New Formulation Exclusivity

The law provides a new use or new formulation marketing exclusivity of three years. This exclusivity applies to new indications for an old drug or new formulations or other labeling changes of an old drug for which the applicant has submitted and obtained approval of a new NDA and which required new clinical trials (but not bioavailability studies) funded by the sponsor of the NDA that were essential to obtain approval.

The new indication can involve the same or a different formulation or dosage as long as it is for a new use of an old drug product. During those three years, the FDA will not approve an ANDA (or paper NDA) for that new indication. However, the FDA could accept the filing of an ANDA (or paper NDA) during the three-year period and thus the ANDA could be approved by the end of the third year. The FDA will also approve a new NDA during the three year period; however, it is unlikely that anyone would attempt to prepare and file a full NDA for the same indication since they would only have to wait for three years to copy it with an ANDA filing and preparing and filing a full NDA would take longer and cost much more.

(d) Pediatric Exclusivity

The pediatric exclusivity adds six months marketing exclusivity to *all* the other exclusivities for the approved active drug as well as effectively adding six months to the expiration dates of patents listed for the drug product in the FDA Orange Book. While the patent terms are not actually extended, the FDA acts as if they were and will not approve ANDAs (or paper NDAs) until the extended date is met. The award of six months applies only to patents and exclusivities in place when the pediatric exclusivity is granted. The pediatric exclusivity applies to the active drug moiety, so that a related product or improved product containing the same active drug moiety also receives the pediatric extension.

A pediatric exclusivity is possible only if the FDA makes a request for a clinical study to be done in children and that it is done in accordance with FDA's instructions. The study does not need to be successful in order to be eligible for the six month exclusivity. If an ANDA has been submitted and is ready for approval after the pediatric study has been submitted to FDA, but before FDA has accepted it, FDA may hold up the ANDA approval for up to 90 days while it is reviewing the submission for approval. Under a new statute, the FDA can now require NDA holders to perform pediatric studies.

(e) 180-Day Generic Product Exclusivity

The 180-day generic product exclusivity was originally intended to encourage patent challenges to listed drugs by giving challengers what was thought to be a modest incentive to invalidate any patent(s) covering the listed drug product and therefore compensate the generic company for its costs in invalidating an improperly granted patent.

In practice, this modest incentive has become the single most important motivator for the generic industry because the first generic drug on the market typically obtains and maintains the majority of sales of that product indefinitely and more importantly, the profit made during that first 180-day period often exceeds the profit made for the rest of the life of the generic product. The reason for this is that in the absence of competition from other generic drugs, the first generic company does not significantly lower the price of the innovator drug during the six months exclusivity period which results in huge profits based on the minimum investment required to copy the innovator.

As a result of this single incentive, the patents covering most major drug products in the U.S. are being challenged earlier and earlier since generally only the first to file an ANDA with a paragraph IV certification challenging a patent for the listed drug is eligible for the 180-day exclusivity. As a result, the validity of virtually all major patented drugs is being challenged not necessarily because they are not meritorious patents, but only because that is the road to riches. Thus major generic companies have scores of such suits ongoing and generic companies rely on the law of averages—if you place enough bets, you are sure to win a few of them and the cost of each bet is relatively low while the payout is enormous, so the more bets the better the return. The innovators are fighting back with innovative strategies of their own and those strategies are further explained in Chapter 7 on life-cycle management.

How does one become eligible for the 180-day exclusivity? Under current law, which was recently amended by the Medicare Act (more on that later), the first generic drug manufacturer to file a substantially complete ANDA for a drug product listed in the Orange Book and who also challenges at least one listed patent in the Orange Book for that drug product by filing what is called a Paragraph IV certification is eligible for a 180-day exclusivity period. During that 180-day period the FDA may not approve another ANDA for the same drug product for the same indication.

In this context "same drug product" means the exact same drug product including dosage form so that an ANDA filed for a 5 mg tablet of a given drug product would only prohibit FDA from approving another ANDA during the 180-day period for the same 5 mg tablet and thus the FDA would be free to approve another company's ANDA for a 10 mg tablet of the same active drug for the same indication.

The 180-day period starts when the generic drug is first commercialized in the U.S. However, under current law, the 180-day exclusivity period can be forfeited for a number of reasons:

1 If the generic drug is not sold within 75 days after the ANDA is approved or within 30 months after the ANDA is filed, whichever is earlier, or within 75 days from a final decision that the patent is invalid or not infringed, it is forfeited.

2 If another ANDA applicant obtains a final judgment invalidating the challenged patent, the first ANDA applicant must begin commercial marketing within 75 days, or else it is forfeited.

3 If the ANDA applicant withdraws its ANDA, or amends or withdraws its Paragraph IV certification, it is forfeited.

4 If the ANDA applicant enters into an agreement with either the NDA holder or another generic company, which agreement is determined by the FTC or a court to be anti-competitive, it is forfeited.

5 If all the patents for the listed drug product expire before the generic is marketed, it is forfeited.

Interestingly, if an ANDA applicant forfeits his 180-day exclusivity, the second ANDA filer to meet all the requirements does *not* become eligible for the 180-day exclusivity. Also, if two ANDA filers for the same listed drug file on the same day, the FDA currently takes the position that both are "first to file" so that they would both get the 180-day exclusivity. A current practice of the smaller generic companies today is to "share" their 180-day exclusivity with a large generic company and share profits.

The rule changes in the 180-day exclusivity brought about by the Medicare Act apply to ANDAs filed after December 8, 2003. For ANDAs filed on or before that date, the old rules apply. The one change that is retroactive makes clear which court decision triggers the exclusivity period (this was ambiguous under the old law). It is now a final decision by a District Court if there is no appeal or it is a final decision of the Court of Appeals (CAFC) if it is appealed.

As a practical matter, the 180-day exclusivity may not in fact be exclusive. That is because the owner of the listed or branded drug can license a so-called "authorized generic" to a generic company or to its own generic division to compete with the generic company who obtained the 180-day exclusivity. Because consumers now have more choices, all sellers of the product must lower prices to stay competitive. Generic companies have challenged this practice in the courts and before the FDA on the grounds that it defeats the purpose of the Hatch Waxman 180-day exclusivity. The FDA has replied that authorized generics lower drug prices to consumers and therefore they are consistent with the intent and goals of the Hatch Waxman Act. (One could conclude from this that the generic companies' often stated belief in the value of competition and resulting lower prices for consumers is muted only when their own exclusivity is threatened). In fact, just as the rise of generic drugs has increased competition and lowered drug prices to consumers, the rise of authorized generics similarly provides lower cost drug products to consumers. More on authorized generics in Chapter 7.

4. Other Exclusivities

Other common forms of exclusivity are trade dress, trademarks and trade secrets. Of these, the most common for pharmaceuticals is trade dress in the form of tablet shape, size and color.

Generally, trade dress refers to the non-functional appearance of a product or its packaging including the shape or design of the product itself. If a trade dress also satisfies the requirements for trademark protection, it can be trademarked as well. One example would be the glass bottle used for many years by Coca Cola®. Its unique shape acquired distinctiveness and became associated with the source of the product and therefore could be trademarked and Coke® could prevent other soft drinks from using it.

For pharmaceuticals, a number of courts have found that the color, size and shape of tablets are arbitrary and nonfunctional having nothing to do with the product's therapeutic function and therefore may be protected as trade dress if they become distinctive. However, a more recent case (*Shire v. Barr*, CAFC 2003) found that providing similar, but not identical color and shape for drug tablets to treat hyperactivity improved patient acceptance and compliance thereby making them functional and not protectable as trade dress.

In that case, Barr used similar, but not identical shapes and colors for its generic tablets and also used a "b" mark on each tablet, while Shire used the letters AD for Adderall, the brand name of the product. This case suggests that relying on color and shape for distinctiveness and exclusivity is not likely to offer strong protection in the future, except possibly to prevent virtually identical copying of nonfunctional color, shape and marking which could lead to claims of unfair competition by passing off the generic company's tablets as the innovator's.

Trademarks can also offer some protection for prescription drug products over time, especially famous ones such as Viagra® or Botox®. These names will never become generic for a product because the FDA will not allow a generic company to use the trademark to name the generic drug product since the generic must be named by the drug's chemical name. Likewise, the FDA will not let another company use a confusingly similar name either. In this regard, the FDA functions as a mini-trademark office and tries to insure that there will be no incorrectly prescribed drugs because of confusingly similar names. As a result, the FDA pays special attention to the initial letters of a trademark as physicians' writing clarity is famous for its absence in a typical prescription order form.

5. Exclusivity Outside the U.S.

Many countries are more liberal with regulatory exclusivities. In Europe, the current law provides for either six or ten years of marketing exclusivity for a new chemical entity (NCE) with the ten years provided by the larger countries. But that is not the case for improvements. Under a recent ruling by the European Court of Justice in a case brought by Novartis to obtain exclusivity for an improved version of one of its older products, the Court essentially ruled there is no six or ten year exclusivity provided for improvements to drug products. This decision could produce a negative incentive for companies to develop improvements of their existing products if generic companies can copy them as soon as they are launched.

However, there is a new EU directive (regulation 727/2004) that is intended to come into effect on a country-by-country basis no later than November 1, 2005 that will provide a more uniform system of data and marketing exclusivity for Europe for pharmaceutical products filed for approval *after* that date. In this context, "data exclusivity" refers to the period in which a generic company may not *file* a request for a generic copy while "marketing exclusivity" refers to the period in which a generic company may not be *approved* for marketing.

Under the new regulations, a new chemical entity or NCE will be entitled to eight years of data exclusivity plus two additional years of marketing exclusivity plus one additional year of marketing exclusivity based on approval of an improvement if it involves a "significant new indication". The additional year attaches to both the improvement and the original product only if the improvement product is approved within eight years of approval of the original product.

While this may be okay for the original product, it provides very limited exclusivity for the improvement. If the new indications are not deemed "significant", the one-year exclusivity applies only to the improvement. Thus it is clear that the EU has made a policy decision not to encourage improvements of pharmaceutical products, but instead to favor generics of older products. There is also a one-year exclusivity for switches to OTC status from a well-recognized prescription product, which is intended to encourage OTC switches since the government does not reimburse OTC drugs. There is also a ten-year exclusivity for orphan drugs that is an important regulatory exclusivity. The ten new accession countries have asked for more time to implement these new rules.

To take advantage of these new rules, a new drug must be filed using the centralized procedure *after* the date for national implementation, i.e., November 1, 2005. For drugs approved or filed before that date, the old rules apply. There is also a proposal to add a U.S. type of pediatric exclusivity of six months, but that has not yet been approved.

Japan provides data exclusivity for NCEs of six years, with improvements entitled to four years. Canada provides no effective regulatory exclusivity.

6. Exceptions to Regulatory Exclusivities

There are some classes of products in the U.S. that are not eligible for data or marketing exclusivity. Medical devices are not eligible nor are older antibiotics. Congress passed a law some time ago that placed antibiotics in a special regulatory category. Then more recently, that special category was done away with for future antibiotics, but the law was maintained for certain specified older antibiotics. As a result, patents covering those older antibiotics are not eligible to be listed in the Orange Book and therefore they are not eligible for any regulatory exclusivity, and ANDAs do not have to file patent certifications and therefore innovators typically do not get the opportunity to file patent infringement suits under the Hatch Waxman Act before ANDAs for these old antibiotics are granted since ANDA filings are maintained in confidence by FDA. However, if an innovator finds out about an ANDA filing for one of those products, it has the right to sue the generic company for patent infringement, though there is no 30-month period put in place during which FDA cannot approve the ANDA.

Two recent suits are now pending which have challenged the FDA's rigid interpretation of this legislation and have requested access to the Orange Book for patents covering new uses and new formulations of two of the older drugs listed as antibiotics for new uses or indications which have nothing to do with killing microbiological agents.

Biologicals, such as biotech and vaccine products, are also not eligible for these regulatory exclusivities, except for the Orphan Exclusivity of seven years. But before you ask your Congressman to look into this, recall that biologicals are not subject to becoming generics at this time so they don't really need the exclusivity protection. If the law changes to allow generic biologicals, appropriate exclusivity for biologicals should be provided.

Take Home Message

There are six regulatory exclusivities in the U.S.

- Orphan drug: 7 years.
- New Chemical Entity (NCE): 5 years.
- New use or new formulation: 3 years.

- Pediatric: 6 months.
- First-to-file generic exclusivity: 180 days.
- First-filer generic exclusivity is a significant incentive for generic companies to seek to invalidate patents covering innovative drugs, but it can also be forfeited.
- Authorized generics from innovators are tending to reduce the value of the first-filer 180-day exclusivity.
- European exclusivity rules are more generous and currently provide 6-10 years for NCEs, but nothing for improvements.
- New rules for Europe effective in November, 2005 provide a maximum of 11 years of exclusivity for NCEs, 10 years for orphan drugs and one year for new uses or OTC switches.
- Japan provides 6 years of exclusivity for NCEs and 4 years for certain improvements.
- Older antibiotics, biologicals and medical devices are not entitled to any regulatory exclusivity, except that biologicals may qualify for Orphan exclusivity.

The previous chapters have discussed patents and FDA and regulatory exclusivity. The next Chapter discusses the **Hatch Waxman Act**. This law is the third leg of the life-cycle management stool and *integrates* the two separate disciplines of patents and regulatory into one interrelated discipline.

CHAPTER 6

Hatch Waxman Act

1. Historical Background

The Hatch Waxman Act was enacted in 1984 as a result of a tacit agreement between the established innovator drug industry and an emerging generic drug industry to solve both of their problems. The generic industry was unhappy because a recent court decision, *Roche v. Bolar*, had established that a generic company could be sued for patent infringement for doing the testing necessary to file an ANDA before the patent expired, so that patent terms were being effectively extended since it takes two to three years to do the required testing and obtain approval and that would now all have to be done after patent expiration.

On the other hand the innovator companies were unhappy because regulatory requirements were taking longer and longer to meet and significant portions of the patent life of the drugs were being lost. And Congress wanted to make available cheaper forms of drugs that were no longer covered by patent and wanted to overrule the *Bolar* decision.

So the industries and Congress hit upon a compromise which would allow the generic industry to be able to do the testing while the patent was still in force so they could sell generic products the day the patent expired. In exchange, the innovator companies would be able to get the terms of their patents extended to make up for some of the patent term lost because of the required regulatory testing for approval. In addition, the generic industry would be able to rely on the safety and efficacy data for the drug product filed with the FDA by the innovator, so long as it could establish they were "the same" as the innovator drug (more on that later).

The new law also gave the generic industry the opportunity to challenge the innovator's patents prior to going on the market to avoid the risk of payment of significant damages if the patent was upheld. At the same time, it also allowed the innovators to keep generic products off the market while the patent was being tested in court and off the market until the patent expired if it was upheld.

Henry Waxman, Democratic Congressman from California and Oren Hatch, Republican Senator from Utah, sponsored the non-contentious "Drug Price Competition and Patent Term Restoration Act of 1984" and both industries and Congress thought they got what they wanted. Now 20 years later, things are more contentious and in addition a number of changes to the law have recently been made.

2. The Law Today

The following is a summary of the current law, but first two definitions to help explain the law. A brand name drug is sold under a *proprietary* name (commonly called a brand name) and promoted by the brand owner, e.g., Advil® or Tylenol®, while a generic drug is sold under its *established* name (commonly called its "generic" name) and is typically not promoted, e.g., ibuprofen or acetaminophen. (These examples are OTC and not prescription products, but you get what I mean). There are also so-called "branded generics" which are differentiated generic products promoted under a brand name.

Generally under Hatch Waxman, FDA will approve a generic drug in the form of an Abbreviated New Drug Application or ANDA if the generic company establishes that its product is pharmaceutically equivalent and bioequivalent to the drug it wants to copy. "Pharmaceutically equivalent" means the generic drug contains the same active drug, uses the same dosage form and strength, and employs the same route of administration and has the same labeling as the innovator or "reference" drug. In order to be substitutable for a branded drug by a pharmacist, a generic company must also prove to the FDA that its generic drug is bioequivalent to the reference drug. To prove bioequivalence, it must be shown that the generic drug will function in the body in the same way as the reference drug.

For example, tablets for oral use typically must establish dissolution times and blood levels of active drug after ingestion that are comparable to the branded drug, but no actual clinical trials may be required. There are exceptions however, e.g., generic products for ophthalmic, otic and parenteral solutions can request a waiver of bioequivalence under FDA regulations, but locally acting drugs (other than otic or ophthalmic solutions) typically require clinicals (testing in humans) to establish bioequivalence.

When a generic company files its ANDA, it must also make a patent certification if there are any patents covering the branded or reference drug product listed in the Orange Book. As you may recall from Chapter 4 on the FDA, the Orange Book is where the innovator companies are required to list their patents for the branded or reference drug products.

3. Patent Certifications

There are four different patent certifications that can be made and the ANDA filer must make one of the following with respect to the Orange Book:

    I   that there is no patent information listed,
    II that there is a listed patent, but it is expired,

III that the listed patent will expire on a stated
date, or

IV that the listed patent is invalid or will not be
infringed.

If the ANDA filer makes one of the first two certifications, FDA can approve the ANDA when it is ready to
do so. If the ANDA filer makes the third certification,
the FDA provides a "tentative approval" of the generic
drug that becomes effective on the day the patent
expires. The fun starts when the generic company
makes the so-called "Paragraph IV certification".

If the ANDA filer makes a Paragraph IV certification,
he must notify the patent owner(s) and the owner of the
NDA for the drug product (which may or may not be the
same person) within 20 days of filing the ANDA and
provide a detailed statement of the legal and factual
grounds that the patent is not valid or not infringed.

4. Suits Following Patent Certification

Under Hatch Waxman, the patent owner has the
right to file suit in Federal Court against the ANDA
filer for infringement of the patent if he does so within
45 days of receipt of the Paragraph IV certification. If
suit is filed, the FDA is prevented by law from approving the ANDA for 30 months from the date of receipt of
the notice by the patent owner and NDA owner. The
30-month period can be shortened if the Court rules
that the patent is invalid or unenforceable in less than
30 months. If the patent holder does not file suit within the 45-day period, the FDA may approve the generic
product at any time.

Generally, it is in the patent owner's best interests
to file suit following receipt of the Paragraph IV certification, though not always. Another strategy might be
not to take advantage of the Hatch Waxman rules that
permit suit to be filed before the infringing generic
product is launched, but to wait to see if the infringing

generic product is approved and launched and if so, sue for actual damages, e.g., lost profits. Under these conditions, a generic company has to think twice about launching the generic drug since its profits are typically less than the drug owner's profits and damages (i.e., lost profits to the innovator drug company), could exceed the generic product's sales, especially when actual damages could be as much as trebled with a finding of willful infringement.

However, the patent owner typically sues following receipt of the Paragraph IV certification to try to keep the infringing product off the market and to avoid the risk of potential disruption in the marketplace and lowered innovator company's sales and earnings and stock price that typically occurs when a generic product replaces a significant branded product.

If the innovator company files suit, a judge rather than a jury usually hears the case. It is typically resolved within the 30-month period by the patent being either held valid and infringed, or invalid or unenforceable due to some defect in the patent. If the patent is upheld, the Court will order the generic company to stay off the market until the patent expires and the FDA will not be able to finally approve the ANDA until the patent expires and all of the regulatory exclusivities, including the pediatric, have expired. Since the generic product is not on the market, there is no claim for damages allowed other than attempts to get attorneys fees reimbursed. The CAFC has recently ruled that the mere filing of an ANDA cannot be grounds for alleging willful infringement which was a rationale previously given for getting attorneys' fees awarded (*Glaxo v. Apotex*, CAFC 2004).

If the patent is held invalid by the Federal District Court, the FDA is free to approve the generic product and the generic company is free to sell it. However, the innovator company may also appeal the decision of the lower court to the Court of Appeals for the Federal

Circuit (CAFC) in Washington, DC, the only appeals court for patent cases. If the CAFC reverses the lower court and upholds the patent, the generic company will be subject to damages for infringement if it has placed the generic product on the market. This puts a big risk on the generic company to decide whether to sell "at risk" during the period of the appeal. Generic companies often wait until the appeal decision has been handed down to avoid that risk, though lately they have become more aggressive and may launch the generic product after a favorable lower court ruling if they believe the decision will be affirmed. However, with the new rule providing that the 180-day exclusivity does not start until a decision by the CAFC, first-filers will likely wait for that decision before selling the generic product.

5. Medicare Act Amendments

In December of 2003, some amendments to Hatch Waxman were signed into law as the Medicare Prescription Drug Improvement and Modernization Act (the "Medicare Act"). The Medicare Act provides a number of important new rights and limitations including the following:

- limits drug companies to a single 30-month stay,
- Significantly amends the rules about the 180-day exclusivity for the first-filer generic company,
- provides a right to generic companies to bring a declaratory judgment of patent infringement if the brand company fails to bring suit after a Paragraph IV certification,
- allows a generic filer to challenge the propriety of an Orange Book listing if it was sued after providing a Paragraph IV certification on a patent it did not think should have been listed in the Orange Book, and

- provides that agreements between generic companies (who have provided Paragraph IV certifications) and innovators relating to the manufacturing, marketing or sale of the drug in question or market exclusivity must be filed with the Department of Justice and the Federal Trade Commission (FTC).

(a) 30-Month Stay

Regarding the 30-month stay, innovator companies had been listing additional patents in the Orange Book long after the reference drug was approved and *after* they had received Paragraph IV certifications. These so-called "late listed" patents sometimes covered off-label indications (uses of the drug which were not approved by FDA, but which doctors were commonly prescribing the drug for), metabolites or various crystal structures and hydrates of the drug, and other variations on the active drug such as novel characteristics of the drug product formulation.

As a result, generic companies were subject to multiple 30-month periods as the innovator company was entitled to a 30-month period for each late-listed patent, since the generic company was required to provide a Paragraph IV certification for each one listed in the Orange Book whether or not the generic company thought the listing was proper. The new law is intended to provide a single 30-month period by restricting the 30-month stay only to patents that were listed in the Orange Book *prior* to the filing of the ANDA.

(b) 180-Day Exclusivity

Regarding the 180-day exclusivity for generic companies, the law before the Medicare Act had some flaws. Since the previous law awarded this important exclusivity to the first-filer, generic company employees would have to line up outside the FDA days and even weeks before the first day an ANDA could be filed to try to be first to obtain first-filer status. To stop this practice, the FDA issued a guidance that it would consider all filers who filed a complete ANDA on the same day to be "first-filers". The Medicare Act made this law.

In addition, the previous law applied separately to each listed patent. As a result, a generic company who filed an ANDA after the first-filer, but who was the first to file a Paragraph IV certification against a different or "late listed" patent, was also entitled to the 180-day exclusivity. This led to confusion and even litigation between different generic companies to establish which one was entitled to the 180-day exclusivity and when it would start. The new law simplifies this by applying the 180-day exclusivity on a *product* instead of *patent* basis, so there is only one 180-day exclusivity per drug product and that is granted to the generic company(s) that is first-filer for the product.

In addition the new law affects agreements between generic companies and branded companies intended to restrict the transfer of the 180-day exclusivity. Now, the first "commercial marketing" that triggers the 180-day period is not restricted to the first sale of an ANDA product, but is also triggered by the sale of the innovator drug as an "authorized generic", e.g., in a supply agreement between a generic company and a branded company. See Chapter 7 for more on authorized generics and how they are significantly changing the landscape for generic companies.

The new law also requires any "deals" between innovators and generic companies that have filed a Paragraph IV certification must be reported to the FTC and Department of Justice. This was an attempt to put some sunlight on the now challenged past practices of some innovator and generic companies entering into settlements of Hatch Waxman patent litigation in which the innovator made payments to the generic company to settle the case, leaving the innovator's product on the market with no generic product competition. The result of this legislation also makes settlements of such litigation much more difficult to enter into since any compromise in which a generic company receives something of value in exchange for dropping even a questionable suit has the potential of being considered improper by the authorities if the generic company agrees to delay entry into the market for any substantial period.

Finally, the new law settled an issue about which court decision triggered the start of the 180-day period. Previously, the FDA had taken the position it was a "final" ruling and that required a ruling from the Court of Appeal. A later Court case concluded that the language of the statute meant any ruling and so the trigger was the District Court decision. This created a big problem for the first-filer because the 180-day exclusivity would be over before the appeal was decided. The new law makes it clear the trigger is a final decision by the District Court if there is no appeal or by the CAFC if it is appealed.

(c) Declaratory Judgment Actions

The new law also adds a new right for generic companies to file a declaratory judgment ("DJ") action against the innovator if the innovator does not sue the generic company for patent infringement within the 45-day period provided after the generic company files the Paragraph IV certification. The generic industry wanted this right in the event the innovators did *not* sue them in response to a Paragraph IV certification, because this put the generic industry at risk of suit when it obtained approval and manufactured and launched the product. The generic industry wanted the right to have the patent litigation resolved before the generic product was approved. In order to file such a DJ action, a generic company must also provide confidential access to its ANDA so that the innovator can assess whether the generic product is infringing. No such confidential access is required if the

Paragraph IV certification only relates to patent invalidity.

However, it is unclear at this time whether the new legislation will in fact afford the generic industry any additional rights, for the reason that courts traditionally do not allow such DJ actions on constitutional grounds, unless there is an actual case or controversy. This generally requires that a generic company establish that it is in "reasonable apprehension" of being sued for patent infringement. If the innovator is careful not to make any threats towards the generic company, the courts will not be likely to allow such DJ actions.

Two recent related cases illustrate an evolving litigation strategy involving the foregoing. Warner-Lambert (now Pfizer) sued Teva pharmaceuticals after receiving a Paragraph IV certification in a typical Hatch Waxman suit over a generic challenge to the innovative drug Accupril®. Teva was the first-filer and thus was entitled to the 180-day exclusivity if it won. In June, 2004, the Federal District Court in New Jersey held the patent valid and infringed.

In the meantime, eight additional generic companies had filed ANDAs for the same drug. However, when Pfizer received their Paragraph IV certifications, it did an interesting thing. It did nothing. In response, TorPharm, one of the eight generic companies, brought an action against Pfizer for a declaratory judgment (DJ) that the Accupril patent was invalid.

TorPharm argued that based on the new amendments to the Hatch Waxman Act under the Medicare Act, TorPharm did not have to meet the traditional requirements for a DJ action. The Federal District Court in Delaware disagreed and ruled against TorPharm saying that the constitutional requirements for a DJ action had not changed and that Pfizer had made no threats of suit against TorPharm and TorPharm was not under a reasonable apprehension of being sued and therefore the Court had no jurisdiction to hear the DJ action.

This may be a very smart approach to one of the problems of multiple litigations. A patent can be held valid any number of times, but a new infringer can always challenge it again. However, once a patent is finally held invalid, it is *invalid* for all. So there is a certain risk in multiple litigations, not to mention the cost and time involved, since somewhere along the line a judge or jury could hold a patent invalid, and therefore it is better to minimize the times at bat.

In this Case, Pfizer now has a ruling its patent is valid and has positioned itself so it won't have to re-litigate the patent unless one of the eight generic companies decides to launch the generic. Then they will be in the tough position of having to defeat a patent that has already been upheld and pay Pfizer's lost profit damages if they don't succeed. Pfizer is apparently betting no one will be willing to do this, so it will be interesting to see if this strategy works.

(d) Counterclaim to De-list

Finally the new law provides that a generic company can counterclaim to de-list a patent that it thinks should not have been listed in the Orange Book. This was intended to provide the generic industry with the right to challenge Orange Book listings as previous court decisions indicated they could not be challenged and the generic industry thought that encouraged listing of frivolous patents. This new right is limited as it cannot be brought independently (only as a counterclaim to a suit by the innovator) and the only remedy allowed is de-listing of the improperly listed patent, i.e., no money damages allowed.

(e) Canada

The only other country to have a similar statute as Hatch Waxman is Canada. In Canada the innovator company is similarly allowed to list its patents covering its approved drug products in a government registry and ANDA filers in Canada must likewise provide notice to innovator companies if they intend to challenge the listed patents. Innovator companies can likewise file suit for infringement within a defined period (50 days) and if they do, the Canadian health authorities may not approve the ANDA for two years, unless a court decides the patent is invalid before the two-year period is up.

A curious aspect of this procedure in Canada is that while the law in Canada requires a generic company to send the equivalent Paragraph IV certification (called a Paragraph 5 letter in Canada), it does not have to be truthful, based on a recent Canadian Court of Appeals decision (*Syntex and Allergan v. Apotex*, 2003). Thus the generic company apparently may legally shade the fact that it is infringing a patent by, for example, making untrue or ambiguous statements about the formulation of its product. If the innovator fails to sue for infringement within the time provided, the innovator company has no right to sue under the statute after the time for suit had passed and that any alleged fraud or misrepresentation must be addressed in a separate suit for patent infringement after the generic product has been approved and launched. This places every innovator company in Canada in the odd position of having to sue every generic company that sends a notice letter since the notice letter does not have to be truthful. This is an example of how Canada favors generics over innovators.

Canada also has the same requirement that patents must be listed within 30 days of grant with the health authorities in Canada. However, in Canada this is set in stone and if the innovator company misses this date by even one day, the right to receive the ANDA filing notice from the generic company is lost. This is actually a burden on the innovator company to accomplish consistently since it has to have close coordination between its Canadian patent agents and its internal patent and regulatory departments in order to get this done within the short time permitted.

On the other hand, there is no restriction in Canada to filing additional patents after the generic company has sent its first patent notification to the innovator. If an additional patent is listed, the generic company must send another notification and the innovator is entitled to sue again and gets another 2 years in which the Canadian FDA cannot approve the generic drug. In addition, while there is some disagreement about this, innovators are listing patents covering off-label uses of their drugs. Suit is then filed based on the testimony of physicians that they use the innovator product off-label for the patented off-label use and would do the same with the generic drug if it were approved and sold. Both of these practices were common in the U.S. during the last five years, but are no longer allowed in the U.S. under current laws and regulations.

Take Home Message

- The Hatch Waxman Act provides generic companies the right to copy innovator's drugs after certain defined exclusivity periods have elapsed and provides innovators patent term extensions of up to five years to make up for time lost in obtaining approval to market from FDA.
- A generic company must make a patent certification as part of an ANDA or 505(b)(2) filing.
- A Paragraph I or II certification means the FDA may approve the ANDA when it is ready.

- A Paragraph III certification means the FDA will approve the ANDA when the last listed patent in the Orange Book expires.
- A Paragraph IV certification means that the generic company is either alleging non-infringement of all listed patents or challenging the validity of one or more of the listed patents in the Orange Book.
- An innovator has 45 days from receipt of a Paragraph IV certification to sue the generic company for infringement.
- If suit is filed, the FDA is barred from approving the ANDA for 30 months or for any such shorter period if a District Court rules on the patent challenge in less than 30 months.
- Medicare Act Amendments allow only one 30-month period for each ANDA or 505(b)(2) filed and off-label use patents may not be listed in the Orange Book.
- Certain types of agreements between generic companies and innovators must be reported to the Justice Department and FTC.
- Canada has a similar statutory scheme and bars the health authorities from approving a generic drug for two years from the patent certification date, but more than one such two-year period may be obtained.

The next Chapter discusses how to use the information previously developed on patents, FDA, regulatory exclusivity and the Hatch Waxman Act to bring about **Product Life-Cycle Management**.

CHAPTER 7

Putting it All Together: Product Life-Cycle Management

In view of the right of generic companies to copy innovators and obtain approvals of generic drugs in the absence of patent protection after the limited exclusivity periods described in previous chapters have expired, brand name drug owners have developed strategies to protect their long term investments and current sales. These strategies are known generally as product life-cycle management and are intended to extend the life of innovator products. Professionals involved in strategic marketing also have developed a number of non-product oriented techniques to enhance a product's success, but the focus of this chapter will be on product life-cycle management by use of patents, regulatory strategies, product improvements and the Hatch Waxman Act.

Generally, life-cycle management or LCM starts early and ideally is integrated into the entire development cycle itself. That is, even before the product has been developed, the people responsible for development and marketing must have in mind the need to provide an adequate life to the product. LCM involves a number of interactive strategies designed to enhance product life through the primary forms of exclusivity available to pharmaceutical products, through an interactive mix of patents, product improvements, FDA exclusivity and FDA rulings through Citizen Petitions, all at different stages in the product life cycle.

1. Patents

A product life cycle begins in the initial discovery of a promising lead compound. The first patents are intended to cover the general chemical family or genus of compounds; so patent claims are directed broadly to cover the genus as well as narrowly to cover the lead compound and variations in-between. The main emphasis is on the chemical side—identifying chemical structures and methods of manufacturing them.

(a) Development Stage

During the development stage where the pre-clinical, pharmacological and other biological aspects of the lead compound are evaluated, additional patents can be filed on newly discovered medical uses and novel formulations for the drug to enhance efficacy or to overcome drug metabolism or drug delivery issues. Improved methods of manufacture may be developed at that time for scale-up in preparation for clinical trials.

(b) Clinical Stage

During the clinical stage, where the drug is tested in humans, additional patents can be filed on new dosage forms, methods of administration, potential new uses which may come to the attention of clinicians as side effects (which was how Viagra® was discovered) and possible novel drug combinations with other known drugs. Pharmacokinetic data can also reveal patentable aspects of drugs, e.g., a pH change in an ophthalmic solution can unexpectedly enhance drug absorption through the cornea allowing a lower concentration of active drug resulting in reduced side effects. During this period, additional drug forms also may be identified, such as active metabolites or stereoisomers of the drug having unique characteristics, and polymorphs of the drug such as different crystal structures or hydrates (combinations of the solid drug with water).

(c) Line Extensions, New Uses and Formulations

While the drug is pending approval, there is time to think about line extensions, potential new medical uses, improved formulations for better drug delivery such as sustained release formulations or once-a-day administration and improvements in the bulk synthesis of the active drug. Once approved and sold, shortcomings of the drug formulation relating to patient acceptance may come to light that were not apparent from the clinical trials. At this point, an improved formulation may be started to overcome the shortcoming. In addition, work may start on a single isomer improvement or drug combinations with other active drugs.

These techniques typically are applied to innovator drugs, but the same concept applies to a paper NDA drug filing under 505(b)(2) which involves some minor change in the innovator drug or its formulation that may be patentable itself. An example of this is Alcon modifying a patented formulation of an improvement of an innovator ophthalmic drug sold by Merck (Timolol® XE) by using a different gelling agent to get around Merck's patent on its once-a-day drug formulation and at the same time patenting its own new formulation to prevent ANDAs being obtained on its product.

(d) Patent Term Extensions

Finally, any patent term extension that is available for the product should be filed and obtained worldwide. Typical extensions of up to five years are obtainable in the U.S. as well as Europe, Japan, Australia and other countries. The rules in each country vary, but each country provides formulas to make up for some, but not all of the patent time lost while the drug is going through the required regulatory approval hurdles.

In the U.S. the formula adds a maximum extension of five years to the original patent life, but not longer than 14 years of patent life from date of approval of the drug. The actual term is computed by a formula that applies to the period between IND filing and FDA approval of the NDA. The formula basically provides a day for every day the FDA is working on the file and a half-day for every day the applicant is working on the file. Typical patent term extensions are in the range of two to four years. The Patent Office confirms the dates submitted by the patent holder with the FDA and awards the patent term extension after publication in the Federal Register for complaints by interested parties.

The patent term extension does not actually extend the term of a patent for all of its claims. The patent term is extended only for the approved drug product. The question arises then what *exactly* is the approved drug product?

In an interesting recent case (*Pfizer v. Dr. Reddy*, CAFC 2004), a generic company, Dr. Reddy, took the position against the innovator, Pfizer, that a different ester of an active drug was not covered by the patent term extension and got a Federal District Court to agree. The industry was up in arms over this because such a ruling would make a mockery of the concept of patent term extension if insignificant changes in the approved drug product would not be covered by the patent term extension. In this case, it did not matter which ester was used for the drug, as the active drug moiety was the same regardless which ester was used. The Court of Appeals overruled the lower court, finding that the "approved drug product" meant the active drug moiety and not the exact chemical form of the approved drug.

The result of this case makes it clear that generic companies will not be able to make slight changes in salts or esters or hydrates of an active drug to get around a patent term extension. In addition improvements by the innovator, which incorporate the same active drug moiety, will be entitled to protection under the original patent term extension and therefore will encourage such improvements.

2. Product Improvements

The heart of LCM is product improvements following the launch of an original new chemical entity or NCE. These product improvements enable the innovator to improve the product at minimal cost compared to developing an entirely new NCE, while at the same time dramatically enhancing the future value of the NCE by providing improved medicines to the public and thereby extending its useful life.

(a) Active Drug Combinations

Suitable improvements fall into a number of well-known categories including new excipients that may be used alone or in combination with new dosage forms or concentrations of the NCE to reduce side effects and/or to enhance patient comfort or compliance. Line extensions, such as formulating combinations of different active drugs, are common in the ophthalmic industry, where drugs are used in combination such as topical steroids combined with antibiotics to treat infection and inflammation. The FDA recently approved a combination of two well-known cholesterol lowering statins giving new life to Merck's Zocor® by combining it with a newer statin sold by Schering-Plough. As Rick said to Louie, in the closing line of Casablanca, "I think this is the beginning of a beautiful friendship."

(b) Single isomers

If the original drug was a racemate (an NCE consisting of two optical isomers – think of it as equal amounts of a left handed and a right handed version of the same chemical compound), a typical improvement is use of one of the isomers alone that sometimes has better biological activity or lesser or fewer side effects relative to the other isomer and the racemate. An example of this is the prescription successor to Prilosec®, named Nexium®, and promoted as the "Purple Pill®", by Astra Zeneca.

(c) New Delivery Systems

New delivery systems are another possibility such as transdermal patches instead of oral delivery and controlled release formulations for oral delivery providing once-a-day dosing verses multiple times a day dosing. Patients find this more convenient and doctors prefer it for improved patient compliance, i.e., the patient will more likely take the proper dose of the drug.

Each of the foregoing product improvements is entitled to a three-year FDA exclusivity if clinical trials were required for FDA approval and of course it is likely that the new formulation, drug entity or delivery system may be patentable. If the improvement provides valuable new benefits, doctors will prescribe the new formulation instead of the old one, and so a generic company will not be able to make much headway in trying to sell the older, less convenient or more difficult to use version of the drug. Even without a patent, the additional three-year exclusivity would extend the life of a product significantly, since typical product life is only about 12-14 years even if the product is patented. (Recall one cannot even get a patent term extension if there is more than 14 years of life remaining on a patent).

(d) Orange Book Listing of Improvement

There is a further interactive effect with FDA and patents on improvements. If the innovator gets a patent on the improvement, the patent must be listed in the Orange Book. If a generic company wants to copy the improvement after the three-year exclusivity (or three and one-half years if a pediatric exclusivity was obtained on the NCE, since the pediatric exclusivity applies to the improvement as well,) it must file another ANDA and another Paragraph IV certification and the innovator can sue again under the Hatch Waxman Act and the FDA is prevented from granting an ANDA on the improvement for another 30 months.

(e) Original Product Replacement

Another strategy is to launch the improvement early enough so that the innovator's superior marketing ability can be used to direct patients and doctors to the improvement to such an extent that the original product loses virtually all of its market before a generic drug is approved. When the generic drug is approved, there is essentially no market for it since all the patients are using the improvement instead. In some cases, e.g., if the improvement relates to improved safety, the original product can be withdrawn from the market making it even more difficult for the generic drug to get market share.

3. Over-The-Counter Strategy

Another strategy is to develop and launch an over-the-counter (OTC) version of the drug just prior to the time the original product's patent life expires as done by Schering-Plough with Claritin® and Astra Zeneca with Prilosec®. This transfers a significant portion of the old prescription market to the new OTC market for the innovator and reduces market size for the generic company.

4. FDA Citizen's Petitions

If there is a concern that the generic drug may be different in such a way that safety or effectiveness is called into question, another avenue is to make objections to the suitability of the generic product with the FDA by filing a Citizen's Petition (CP). These are formal written requests to the FDA to do or not to do something that the FDA is obliged to consider and reply to publicly. Wyeth filed a CP on the suitability of an ANDA for its conjugated estrogen Premarin®. After lengthy deliberations, the FDA agreed with Wyeth and would not approve an ANDA for Premarin, based on its unique formulation that the company said could not be duplicated by a generic product. (Premarin is extracted from the urine of pregnant mares and is a natural hormone complex more like a biological and not readily duplicated chemically.)

5. Authorized Generics

In an interesting recent turn, two major generic companies, Mylan Pharmaceuticals and Teva, filed a CP with the FDA to ban so-called "authorized generics". Authorized generics are generic products that an innovator company licenses to a third party during the 180-day first-filer generic exclusivity period, thereby effectively taking away the exclusivity period from the generic company that had it. The generic industry counts on the 180-day exclusivity period to make large profits and it is a key growth driver. The presence of a second generic product with lower prices effectively reduces their earnings substantially and has the potential to dramatically alter the current innovator/generic equilibrium.

In June, 2004, the FDA denied the CP and confirmed the rights of the innovator companies to sell authorized generic products indicating that the price reductions in the cost of generic drugs it provided was appropriate and in the public interest. Examples of recent authorized generics include the well-known antidepressant Paxil® (license granted to Par Pharmaceuticals by GlaxoSmithKline) and the oral contraceptive Ortho-Tricyclen® (licensed by J&J to Watson Pharmaceuticals) though Barr Laboratories had first-filer exclusivity rights.

The FDA ruling suggests that we may be seeing this LCM tactic become commonplace in the future as innovators attempt to reduce loss of revenue by meeting competition. As a result, we may see more deals between innovators and certain generic companies for authorized generics. However, note that Mylan has renewed its legal challenge to authorized generics, and FDA's decision to allow them, in the Federal District Court in Clarksburg, PA so the jury is still out on the ultimate validity of authorized generics (*Mylan v. FDA, Watson Pharmaceuticals and P&G*, 2004).

6. Examples of Life-Cycle Management

An innovative drug product, Toradol® (ketorolac tromethamine), a non-steroidal anti-inflammatory drug (NSAID), was invented by Syntex (now part of Roche) in the early 1970s and was approved by FDA for treatment of serious pain conditions. It is non-narcotic and non-habit forming and does not cause physical or mental dependence, as narcotics can. It is administered orally or by injection. Syntex filed and obtained patents on the new chemical entity, for its use in treatment of serious pain and on its method of manufacture.

Additional research begun in the late 1970s lead to the discovery that the compound could also be used topically in the treatment of certain eye conditions. A new patent was therefore filed for treatment of conditions of the eye with topical formulations containing ketorolac tromethamine. Syntex researchers then tried to formulate the compound into a commercially acceptable eye-drop and ran into problems obtaining a robust, stable formulation. A number of Syntex formulation scientists worked for several years on the problem and eventually solved it through the use of a special stabilizer that had not previously been used for stabilizing pharmaceutical products. An additional patent was obtained on the ophthalmic formulation

containing the new formulation with the new ophthalmic stabilizer.

The eye drop product was approved by FDA and
launched in 1992 and all three patents were listed in
the FDA Orange Book. The original patent expiration
date of the compound patent was in 1995 and was
extended to 1997 by patent term extension. The term
for the ophthalmic use patent was 2002 and the expiration date of the formulation patent was in 2009. In
addition, the FDA requested that a pediatric study be
done and after its completion, the patent dates were
effectively extended by six months. The new ophthalmic formulation was entitled to a three-year FDA
exclusivity for its new indication/new formulation for
relief of ocular itching due to seasonal allergic con-
junctivitis. After further clinical studies during the
1990s, the product was also approved in 1998 for an
orphan condition, namely, inflammation following
cataract surgery. This entitled the innovator to a
seven-year FDA exclusivity to 2005, but only for that
indication.

A generic company filed an ANDA for the first indication of the product in 2001 and sent a Paragraph IV
certification asserting the formulation patent was
invalid and not infringed. Within the 45-day period
provided, a patent infringement suit was filed against
the generic company and litigation commenced in the
Federal District Court in San Francisco as a bench trial
in front of the Judge, without a jury. As a result, the
FDA was not able to approve the ANDA for the product
for up to 30 months from the date of receipt of the
Paragraph IV certification or until there was a Court
decision.

The trial was completed by the summer of 2003 before the end of the 30 month period; however, the Court had not issued its ruling by the end of the 30 month period in October, 2003.   The Court however extended the 30 month period until the end of 2003 or until it issued its ruling, whichever came first. The District Court ruled in December, 2003 that the formulation patent was valid and infringed (*Syntex and Allergan v. Apotex*, 2003).   Apotex appealed to the CAFC where the case is currently pending on appeal. If the lower Court ruling is upheld, Apotex will not be able to obtain approval for its generic until the patent expiration date in 2009 plus the 6 months pediatric extension.

This example shows how the combination of good patent protection on each new invention, coupled with use of the Orange Book listing, patent term extension and three different FDA exclusivities (new use, orphan and pediatric), have provided a reasonable life to the innovative eye care product and provided the public with a new, innovative medicine for two important eye conditions. Note that the compound and ophthalmic use patents were never challenged. If the formulation patent is upheld on appeal, and there are no further generic challenges, the product will have a life of about 17 years, after which it will become generic. If the formulation patent is ultimately held invalid, it will have a shorter 13-year life.

Hypothetical Example 2- Lack of Initial Patent Protection

A hypothetical example of the application of life-cycle management is a drug with substantial sales, but little or no patent protection. This can happen for a variety of reasons. Here is one example. The active drug compound is discovered and patented in the usual way by the innovator; however, the compound is unsuccessful for its original indication and is set aside by the innovator, as often happens in pharmaceutical drug research, and information concerning it is published. Some years later, compounds like it are found to be useful in a somewhat related indication and the owner licenses the compound to a company interested in the related area. Unfortunately, the prior publication of the information on the compound also mentioned the possibility of using the compound for the related condition, so it is too late to file a patent covering the new use since the publication is prior art and bars a patent on the related condition.

Notwithstanding the lack of patent protection, the licensee decides to go ahead with the development of the compound for the new use and is ultimately successful in obtaining FDA approval, but somewhat later than expected and by that time, the compound patent has expired. The approved product is entitled to a five-year FDA exclusivity period as it is the first approval of the active drug compound for any medical use. However, the compound patent cannot be listed in the Orange Book because it is expired. As a result, the product is likely to have a short life since the law allows a generic company to file an ANDA at the end of the five-year exclusivity, which does not provide sufficient time for the second company to absorb its development costs as well as the royalty due to the licensor for the license to the IND and the pre-clinical and early clinical work done by the original innovator.

If the remaining patent life is less than six years, one is actually better off without a patent since the presence of a patent listed in the Orange Book allows an ANDA to be filed four years after approval. If no patent is listed, the ANDA cannot be filed until five years after approval (or five and one-half years after approval if a pediatric extension is obtained). Since the

FDA can't approve the ANDA until the end of the five years (or five and one-half years with the pediatric extension), the patent having a shorter term than that is of no value and in fact has a negative value as it allows the ANDA to be filed a year earlier.

Once the FDA approval parties are over, the company's strategic marketing people start getting worried. They can see that the product life will be too short and they start to think how that can be remedied. They call in consultants and discuss the matter with in-house scientific and regulatory staff and start to develop a plan to improve the product with the hopes of also improving its poor life cycle.

The first improvement is to do a clinical trial in children that will allow the company to provide the drug product to children and also obtain a 6-month pediatric extension giving the product five and one-half years instead of five years of exclusivity.

The second improvement is to improve patient acceptability. The current drug must be taken four times daily. Patients are not overly pleased with this regimen and doctors are unhappy because patients forget to take the medication and as a result compliance is not good. The company decides that a suitable improvement would be a once-a-day sustained release product that would provide better patient acceptance and better compliance. Work is started immediately and the formulators come up with a novel and unique sustained release once-a-day formulation that is put in the clinic for testing. Five years after the original product is launched, the new product is approved by the FDA following successful clinical trials and a new NDA filing. Several patent applications are filed on the new sustained release formulation, including the novel aspects of the formulation itself as well as new dosing levels resulting from the use of the new formulation and the discovery that the new dosing levels improve efficacy and reduce side effects.

The new once-a-day sustained release product is launched and immediately receives rave reviews from patients and doctors alike. Within a year, over 90% of combined product sales are the sustained release form. As a result, the company decides to withdraw the original product, as scant sales no longer justify the costs of continuing its manufacture. In addition, the new product receives the three-year FDA exclusivity for a new formulation plus six additional months of pediatric exclusivity, based on the original pediatric grant.

By the end of the fifth year from the launch of the original product, the first patents on the new sustained release formulation patent are granted and listed in the Orange Book. These patents are listed under the new product only as they do not cover the original product. As a result, an ANDA for the old product still cannot be filed until the end of the five and one-half year exclusivity period for the original product. In addition, the patent terms are effectively extended for six additional months by virtue of the pediatric exclusivity obtained for the original product.

Several generic companies have been preparing ANDA submissions for the original product and file them at the end of the five and one-half year exclusivity period. They are approved within 12 months (six and one-half years after the original product introduction) and are launched. The market for the improved sustained release product is not affected very much by the availability of the cheaper generic for the original product, as both patients and doctors prefer the improved product. However, it is now available as a lower cost generic drug for those persons or institutions for which lower cost medicines are deemed of greater importance than the benefits of the improved product.

The generic companies are not very happy with the resulting sales however, so they decide to copy the improved sustained release product. After review of the patents filed in the Orange Book, the generic companies conclude that the patents have sufficient flaws that they could be overturned in court so they copy the improved product and do the work necessary to file new ANDAs on the improvement product. They are filed about a year later during the three-year exclusivity period, which is allowed.

After filing, the generic companies provide a Paragraph IV certification to the innovator and the innovator files a patent infringement suit within the statutory 45 days. The filing of the suit automatically prohibits the FDA from approving the new ANDAs for 30 months or until there is a Court decision. In addition, the generic company who is the first filer to challenge the patents is entitled to the 180-day exclusivity if its ANDA is approved. Interestingly, the filing dates of the ANDAs are kept confidential by the FDA, so it is difficult for anyone to find out which company will get the 180-day exclusivity before the first ANDA is approved.

If the generic companies are not successful in overcoming the patents, the Court will rule that the FDA may not approve their ANDAs until the patents and any pediatric exclusivity expire. If the generic companies succeed in overturning the patents, the FDA can approve their ANDAs at any time. However, even if the innovator loses the case in the District Court, a generic company is not likely to launch its copy until the case has been affirmed on appeal, which ordinarily takes about 12 months. This is because the generic company could be liable for lost profits of the innovator if it launched the generic product and then later the case was reversed and the patents upheld. In addition, the 180-day exclusivity period does not start until a final ruling of the Court of Appeals, so the first filer generic company is usually in no hurry anyway.

To do the math, the innovator receives five years exclusivity for the original product, plus six months pediatric exclusivity, plus three years exclusivity for the new sustained release formulation, plus another 6 months pediatric exclusivity, plus 45 days and 30 months for the Paragraph IV certification, plus 12 months for the appeal. This adds up to about 10 or 11 years--a substantial improvement in life cycle over the original product life. The net result of the foregoing is the innovator has significantly added to the useful life of its drug product franchise while providing value and convenience to patients. Of course, if the patents are upheld, the improvement product's life will continue until the patents expire or until a better product comes along.

These examples illustrate the multi-track nature of life-cycle management. There are patent tracks, FDA exclusivity tracks and product improvement tracks. A good life cycle management program uses all three in parallel for redundancy, so that failure of any one track, e.g., loss of patent protection on the original product, will not necessarily result in a short product franchise life cycle.

7. Biogenerics

The field of biogenerics or so-called "follow-on biologics", as the FDA now refers to them, is not yet a reality, but it is coming. The FDA has indicated that the first likely biological products it will consider for generic approvals are the older drugs, recombinant human insulin and human growth hormone. Historically, these drugs were approved as NDAs making them technically more subject to becoming generic drugs than other biotech drugs that were approved under a different legal scheme and were filed as Biological License Applications (BLAs). This is because historically BLAs were for biologically derived vaccines and were under the jurisdiction of a different branch of FDA than the branch responsible for drugs. Recently FDA has transferred some functions of CBER (the biologicals division) to CDER (the drug division) to provide more uniformity for drug and biologic evaluations.

However, the laws for approval of biologicals and drugs are not the same, including the most important distinction that the Hatch Waxman Act applies only to drugs and does not apply to biologicals. Of course, Congress could act to change the law and probably will at some time in the future as cost pressures on health care continue to mount and as biotech drugs get ever more expensive.

When Medicare must foot the bill for drugs and biologicals starting in 2006, it should not take long for the law to change. Goldman Sachs analysts have estimated that the generic biologicals market will be nearly $12 billion worldwide in 2010. Large generic companies such as Teva and Barr Labs are currently focusing on the development of these types of products. Filings for approval of generics will likely come in the form of 505(b)(2) filings. Novartis has already filed a 505)(b)(2) with FDA for generic human growth hormone.

This suggests biotech companies will have to focus on LCM in earnest if they are to maintain their innovative edge in the future.

CHAPTER 8

Conclusions and Final thoughts

Congratulations. All of you are now experts in pharmaceutical product life-cycle management, or certainly compared to the average professional, well informed on the subject. While I have tried to keep the explanation of the subject light and hopefully interesting, it is a serious matter which affects the lives of millions for better or worse. Innovative pharmaceutical companies must be allowed to continue to innovate. The generics industry must be allowed to offer low cost medicines to people who need them. The laws need to maintain the original balance once struck in 1984 with the passage of the Hatch Waxman Act.

1. Longer Exclusivity Terms

U.S. law currently provides a maximum of four or five years of data exclusivity or three to seven years marketing exclusivity for innovative pharmaceutical products. The typical term for exclusivity for a new NCE is only five and one-half years. These terms are too short for a reasonable return on investment and should be doubled to terms more like the new European regulatory exclusivity of 10–11 years. Then a product would be subject to being copied by a generic company unless it had a valid and enforceable patent.

However, the major shortcoming of the new European regulatory exclusivity (not recognizing new medical uses or improved formulations of old NCEs as meriting significant regulatory exclusivity) should also be addressed. Many important therapeutic advances come about from discoveries of new medical indications for older drugs whose safety and side effect profile is well known, which make them excellent new drug candidates.

2. More Uniform Approval Standards Internationally

Another complex issue is drug costs. People believe drug costs are too high and that pharmaceutical companies are making too much money. One of the ways to lower drug costs would be to have more cooperation between governmental drug regulatory agencies around the world. At the present time, with limited exceptions in smaller countries, new drugs must be approved, re-approved and re-approved again in each country or region. The tests necessary to obtain drug approval in the U.S. will not get the same drug approved in Europe or Japan and vice versa. Companies have to spend hundreds of millions of dollars testing and retesting new drugs to satisfy each country's particular requirements. At one time in the past, Japan even required pre-clinical testing to be re-done on Japanese rats!

Thus, drug-testing requirements have many of the attributes of non-tariff barriers to competition. Japan protects its domestic pharmaceutical industry in this way as does the U.S. and Europe. If the major world governments' health authorities would cooperate on *uniform approval requirements*, new drug prices would be lower because development costs would be significantly reduced and people all over the world would have faster access to new and better medicines.

3. Price Control Issues

Another issue concerning the high cost of new drugs is drug price controls in some countries. These countries control the price of drugs to keep prices low for their citizens, but it only works because there are enough countries that either do not control prices or allow sufficiently adequate prices so that innovative drug developers can still profitably develop new drugs. This results in a "free ride" for the citizens of the low priced countries because the drugs could not be developed for the prices allowed; and it is available to them only because other countries allow sufficiently high prices that justify the development costs and risks.

That is why Americans are calling for drug reimportation from Canada, where they see the same drugs that they buy in the U.S. cost less in Canada. That's because Canada has drug price controls and the U.S. generally does not, though there are required discounts and rebates for Medicare and state drug programs like Medicaid. However instead of getting mad at Canada for controlling drug prices, they get mad at the drug companies for what they perceive as price gouging. If those same drug price controls were in effect in the U.S., the drugs in question would probably not have been developed in the first place, so at least there would be nothing to be mad about (except the absence of the new and better drug).

4. Prescribing Generic Drugs More Often

Another way overall drug prices could be kept lower in America is if doctors would prescribe generic drugs more often. Drug companies promote their latest and greatest new generation of drug products that are typically more expensive than the comparable product they previously promoted and sold; especially if the product has now become a generic. These once new drugs did not suddenly become old, inadequate drugs overnight. Even though the latest drugs may offer significant improvements over the older drugs for some, there may not be a significant difference for others.

For example, one of the best proton pump inhibitors ever invented for reducing stomach acid was

Prilosec® (omeprazole), which was invented, developed and sold by Astra Zeneca. At one time, it was the world's leading drug in terms of sales. The patents on Prilosec have expired and the product has become generic and OTC. As part of Astra Zeneca's product life-cycle management plan, it developed and is currently very successfully marketing, as a new product, one of the chemical isomers that make up omeprazole called Nexium®. Nexium may have some benefits over Prilosec, but for many Prilosec would work just as well as Nexium and at a much lower cost. Yet Nexium's sales are growing dramatically. This is a good example of how doctors could lower medicine costs for patients by recommending lower cost Prilosec-OTC or prescribing the generic of Prilosec (omeprazole) instead of prescribing Nexium.

Of course, this is more complicated than it first appears. People and insurance plans can complicate things. Some patients may prefer Nexium because they get prescription drugs at low cost through their insurance plans. If they had to buy Prilosec-OTC, it would cost them more since insurance won't cover OTC products. And you might not be very happy with your GI specialist if he charged you $250 for telling you to use an OTC medication you could have purchased without seeing him.

However, where there is no specific need for the latest and likely more expensive drug, doctors should prescribe the older, more reliable and probably safer drugs that are likely to have become generic. For example, the older anti-inflammatory drug Ibuprofen (Advil) and the latest one, Vioxx, are similarly acting drugs, but Vioxx turned out to have serious safety issues and had to be withdrawn from the market. And while we complain about the cost of new drugs, we generally don't insist our physicians offer us less expensive and possibly safer alternatives and our health insurers don't give us much incentive to do so either. We shop for most things, but typically not for drugs. Could it be, dear Brutus, that the fault lies not in our stars, but in ourselves?

As a closing thought, the innovative pharmaceutical industry, for all its faults, remains a consummate life-affirming and life-enhancing industry. For ourselves and especially for our posterity, we must continue to make every effort to ensure that the innovative pharmaceutical industry continues to survive and prosper.

Glossary of Terms

510K – A form of filing with FDA for approval of a medical device that refers on an existing approval of a similar medical device.

505(b)(2) – A form of filing with FDA for a drug that refers to published data for safety and efficacy. Often used in place of an ANDA for copying an approved drug with some minor changes in the drug formulation or NCE.

Active moiety – The biologically active portion of a drug molecule.

ANDA – Abbreviated New Drug Application, the filing required by FDA for a generic drug approval.

Authorized generic – A generic version of a branded drug commercialized by the owner of the corresponding brand name drug itself or through a third party.

Biological – A biologically derived drug product typically manufactured by a biological process, such as vaccines, toxins and products of biotechnology which must be filed with FDA for approval as a Biological License Application (BLA).

Biogeneric – A generic of a biological drug; also known as a follow-on biologic.

BLA – Biological License Application.

CAFC – Court of Appeals for the Federal Circuit, the court that hears all patent appeals from the Federal District Courts.

CBER – Center for Biologics Evaluation and Research, a division of FDA.

CDER – Center for Drug Evaluation and Research, a division of FDA.

Centralized Procedure – An administrative procedure in Europe for approving new drugs in all European Union (EU) countries by a single review.

Certificate of Free Sale – A document which smaller countries require to allow sales of a prescription drug in that country establishing that the drug is on sale in a larger country such as the U.S. and thus has been found to be safe and effective.

Certificate of Pharmaceutical Product – A new name for a Certificate of Free Sale.

cGLP – Current Good Laboratory Practices.

cGMP – Current Good Manufacturing Practices.

CIP – Continuation-in-part: a type of continuation of a patent application which makes changes in an existing patent application and obtains the benefit of its filing date for the non-changed portion.

Citizen's Petition – A formal written request to FDA requesting an administrative action ruling.

Claim -Numbered paragraphs at the end of a patent which define the patented invention.

Compound patent – A form of patent that claims a compound and is generally the most preferred type of patent claim covering a pharmaceutical product.

CON – Continuation: a type of patent application that is the same as a predecessor patent application and retains its filing date.

Constructive reduction to practice – The filing of a patent application in the U.S. is the legal equivalent to having reduced the invention to practice.

CP – Citizen's Petition.

Data Exclusivity – A period of regulatory exclusivity during which a regulatory agency will not accept an application for a generic drug.

DDMAC – Division for Drug Marketing, Advertising and Communications, a division of FDA.

Dependant claim – A form of patent claim that internally references another claim for part of its content.

DJ – Declaratory judgment.

DMF – Drug Master File.

Doctrine of Equivalents – Non-literal infringement of a patent where there are insubstantial differences between a patent claim and the infringing product or process.

EMEA – European Medicines Agency.

EPO – European Patent Office.

Equivalents – See Doctrine of Equivalents.

Established Name – The formal name given to each drug substance or NCE; commonly known as the generic name.

FDA – U.S. Food and Drug Administration.

Federal District Courts – The U.S. Courts that hear patent infringement cases.

First-Filer – The informal designation given to a generic company that is the first in time to file an acceptable ANDA for a branded drug product, which makes it eligible for the 180-day exclusivity provide by the Hatch Waxman Act. More than one generic company can obtain first-filer status for the same drug.

Formulation patent – A type of patent designed to cover a drug formulation and typically is the narrowest of patents covering drugs products.

Generic drug – A drug product that is a copy of a brand name drug and is approved for sale based on safety and efficacy data developed by the brand drug owner. It is generally substituted by pharmacies for the brand name drug.

GLP – Good Laboratory Practices.

GMP – Good Manufacturing Practices.

Hatch Waxman Act – The common name of the federal law establishing generic drugs and patent term extensions, officially known as the "Drug Price Competition and Patent Term Restoration Act of 1984".

IDE – Investigational Device Exemption: the first filing with FDA for approval to test a Class III medical device in humans.

IND – Investigational New Drug: the first filing with FDA for approval to test a new drug in humans.

Independent claim – A form of patent claim that does not make any reference to another claim.

Inducement of infringement – A type of indirect infringement of a patent in which the infringer induces a third party to directly infringe the patent. Typically asserted against a manufacturer of a drug product with labeling for a medical use covered by a patent.

Infringement – The act of violating the claims of a valid and enforceable patent.

Infringement opinion – A formal legal opinion on whether a product or process infringes a patent. Often obtained prior to litigation by a potential infringer for reliance to avoid a charge of willful infringement.

Interference – A U.S. Patent Office administrative procedure to establish who is the first inventor of a given invention when two or more inventors claim the same invention.

Life-cycle Management – A strategy for extending the useful life of branded medical products, especially pharmaceutical products.

MAA – Marketing Authorization: the term used in the European Union for the form of filing for an approved drug; corresponds to an NDA in the U.S.

Marketing Exclusivity – A period of regulatory exclusivity during which a regulatory agency will not approve a generic application for marketing a drug.

MRP – Mutual Recognition Procedure.

Medical use patent – A type of patent covering the medical use of a drug product; typically, the second best form of patent protection for a pharmaceutical product in-between compound patents and formulation patents.

Mutual Recognition Procedure – An administrative procedure for approving new drugs in the European Union one country at a time.

NCE – New Chemical Entity.

New chemical entity – The name given to a chemical compound that is being used for the first time in a drug product.

NHI – A Japan agency that provides reimbursement prices for approved drugs in Japan.

Non-obvious – Not obvious to one of ordinary skill in the art to which the invention pertains at the time the invention was made: one of the requirements for patentability.

Novel – New: one of the requirements for patentability.

Off-label Use – The use of an approved drug product by doctors to treat a specific disease or condition not approved by FDA for that drug.

OGD – Office of Generic Drugs: a division of FDA responsible for approving generic drugs.

Orange Book – The informal name given to the FDA publication "Approved Drug Products and Therapeutic Equivalents". The Orange Book is where the FDA lists approved drugs and related patent and regulatory exclusivities.

Orphan Drug – A designation given by FDA for a drug product that meets certain criteria including that there are less than 200,000 persons in the U.S. having the disease or condition to be treated. Also available in Europe.

OTC – Over-the-counter: a designation for a drug product that does not require a prescription.

Paper NDA – A filing for drug approval under section 505(b)(2) of the FDA regulations; typically used for filing of a generic product with one or more changes to a branded drug product.

Paragraph IV Certification – A patent certification provided by a generic company to a brand drug NDA owner that states that a patent listed in the Orange Book for the drug product is either invalid or not infringed.

Parallel Trade – Importation and sale of a branded drug in a second country, by a third party not related to the drug product owner, following authorized sale by the drug owner in another country. Also called parallel imports.

Patent Examiner – An employee of a national Patent Office who examines patents for approval.

Patent Office – A governmental Agency responsible for granting and administering patents.

Patent Prosecution – Written correspondence between the patent owner or his attorney and the patent examiner assigned to examine the patent owner's patent application concerning the patentability of the invention submitted.

PDMA – Prescription Drug Marketing Act of 1988.

PDUFA – Prescription Drug Marketing User Fee Act of 1992 that required drug and biologic drug filers to pay fees to FDA for evaluation of their respective NDAs and BLAs.

PDUFA Date – The date the FDA is required to complete its first review of an NDA; generally ten months following acceptance for filing by FDA.

Pediatric exclusivity – A period of exclusivity for drugs listed in the Orange Book that have met certain requirements for testing in children. The period of exclusivity is six months for the drug product that was tested and applies to improvements containing the same active moiety.

Phase I – First study of a new drug in a small number of healthy human patients to establish safety.

Phase II – The second study of a new drug in a moderate number of human patients having the disease or condition to be treated to establish efficacy and dose ranging.

Phase III – The third study of a new drug in a large number of human patients to establish efficacy.

Phase IV – Post marketing studies to further establish safety.

PMA – Pre-marketing Approval filing with FDA for a Class III medical device. Corresponds to an NDA for pharmaceuticals and a BLA for biologicals.

Polymorphs – Different physical forms of the same active drug and includes different crystalline forms, different hydrates, solvates or amorphous forms.

Prior Art – Publications or patents dated prior to the date of invention or dated more than one year prior to the patent filing date and which disclose or suggest the claimed invention.

Proprietary Name – The name given to a drug product by the owner; commonly called the brand name.

Prosecution History Estoppel – A legal concept that limits the application of the doctrine of equivalents based on statements made or narrowing amendments made to the claims during the prosecution of a patent application before the U.S. Patent Office.

Reference Drug – The brand name drug intended to be copied by a generic drug through the filing of an ANDA.

RMS – Reference Member State. The name of the country in the European Union that is the initial country used for the Mutual Recognition Procedure for drug approval.

Submarine patent – A patent that has been pending for a long time in secrecy and which then issues with claims for inventions after those inventions have been incorporated in well established products.

Validity Opinion – A formal legal opinion on the validity of a patent often obtained by a potential infringer as a defense to a claim of willful infringement.

Willful Infringement – A finding by a Court that a party found to have infringed a patent did so intentionally, allowing any damage award to be increased by as much as three times at the discretion of the judge.